WANDERING IN BOWLAND

A walker's guide to the
footpaths and byways of
Bowland.

By A. A. Lord.

ISBN 0 902272 44 6

Published and Printed in England
by Westmorland Gazette,
22 Stricklandgate, Kendal, Cumbria.

The Grey Stone of Trough

Brilliant sunshine
Deep blue sky
Mayflies rising in the heat haze
Crystal clear becks
Soft springy heather
Curlew calling on a breezy May morning
A cool woodland glade
A primrose by a mossy stone
Wood anemones dancing in the wild March wind
A cobbled street
Hanging baskets spilling geraniums over the old stone pub
All yours in Bowland.

CONTENTS

Contents Continued

Photo 1. Marshaw Wyre flowing by Tower Lodge, Trough of Bowland.

BOWLAND

A countryside of clear tumbling becks, of cattle grazing the peaceful riverside pastures, lovely old villages, the beautiful Hodder valley, wild flowers and woodland, grouse amongst the heather, and high wild fells. This is Bowland, locally pronounced Bolland, unspoilt countryside now officially declared an "Area of Outstanding Natural Beauty".

It has probably changed little since Earl Tostig first owned it before the Normans came. There were more trees then, but it has always been scattered woodland with cattle breeding and dairy farming in the valleys, much as it is today. Bowland became a Royal Forest under the Normans who were great huntsmen. Only the king and his lords were allowed to kill deer within the Forest boundary, so as with other Royal Forests there were strict Forest laws and severe penalties for those who broke them.

From Gibbon Bridge the original Forest Boundary followed Hodder and Ribble to Sawley, then north by Ouzel Hall and Threap Green to Brock Thorn and Dob Dale Beck. Threap is an Old English word for a dispute and also appears in Threaphaw Fell further west which suggests that there were disputes about the Forest boundary. The Forest extended north to Lawkland Fell and Bowland Knotts. The large base stone by the roadside is all that now remains of Cross of Greet which once marked the summit of this route north towards Clapham. From here the Forest Boundary went on past Wolfhole Crag following the watershed "as heaven water deals".

The Grey Stone of Trough dated 1897 marked the old county boundary but it is only a newcomer. There are other very old stones here marking the Forest boundary and traces of old mounds along to Fairsnape and Burnslack Fell where the boundary turned south along Dobson's Brook to the Loud. The extent of the Forest decreased over the centuries and it is no longer a Royal Forest. Nowadays the name Bowland is applied more widely, often much more widely than it ought to be.

The Roman Road through Bowland came over Longridge Fell, crossed the Hodder west of Newton, and on over the fells to Lowgill. The road went northwards because the Romans required a quick route to their northern frontier, but after the Romans withdrew the pattern of roadways began to change.

Christianity came to the north in the 7th century. Sawley Abbey was founded in 1147 and by the end of the 13th century the foundations had been laid for Whalley Abbey which was to become wealthy and influential

Lancaster being the principal port as well as the legal and administrative centre, inevitably the road linking Whalley with Lancaster grew in importance. This road followed the Langden Brook and then over the pass which between Sykes and Marshaw is known as the Trough of Bowland. It was along this same route that John Paslew, Abbot of Whalley, travelled to face trial for treason at Lancaster Assizes, to be followed in the 17th century by the Lancashire Witches. This is still the principal route through Bowland. It is popular at weekends and in summer, but is not really a busy road.

The Dunsop valley to the head of Whitendale is 8kms of woodland, riverside and heather. The Langden valley by contrast is rough grassland and bracken with fewer trees and soon climbs up through the heather and peat of Fiendsdale onto Fairsnape and Parlick, and below Parlick is Chipping.
Chipping is a charming village of mostly 17th and 18th century houses and St. Bartholomew's Church. There has been a church on this site probably since before the 11th century but the present one was built in the 16th century. Chipping means a market and comes from the Old English word for barter. Being just outside the Forest boundary Chipping was an important market centre for the cattle and dairy produce of Bowland. Northeast of Chipping is the Forest village of Slaidburn. This lovely stone village with its old church and school was the administrative centre of the Forest and here the court was held to enforce the Forest Laws.
From its source near Cross of Greet the River Hodder flows by pasture and meadowland through the centre of the Forest of Bowland, below Slaidburn and Newton, past the little village of Dunsop Bridge and through the wooded gorge of Whitewell, then on again by peaceful riverside woodland to Doeford Bridge and Chaigley, all of it beautiful and unspoilt countryside.
Bowland has long walks on ancient ways, Garstang through Calder Vale and the Langden valley to Slaidburn, or up the Whitendale valley and over Salter Fell to Hornby and Wray. There are shorter walks too around Abbeystead, Bleasdale, Chipping, Slaidburn, the Hodder valley and many more.
This is a book to help you to enjoy them all, following the Dipper on a riverside walk, strolling by peaceful sunlit summer meadows or striding through the wild solitude of the remote uplands. Whatever your choice, here is a place to set aside cares and frustrations and relax amidst the beauty that is Bowland.

Photo 2. Sykes Farm, Trough of Bowland

THE ACCESS AREAS

Lancashire County Council have negotiated agreements with some landowners and access areas are now provided at Clougha, Little Gragg and Baines Cragg on Map 4; at Fairsnape on Map 19; at Wolf Fell and Saddle Fell on Map 20; and an access strip 12 metres wide which goes from Grit Fell to Tarnbrook on Maps 2 & 3. Maps and Bylaws are posted up at the usual access points and leaflets about the access areas can be had from the Estates Dept., Lancashire County Council, Winckley Square, Preston. The agreements grant the right to walk over these areas and also protect the landowner's interests which are mainly sheep rearing and grouse shooting. For this reason dogs are not allowed and no fires or stoves are to be lit because of the considerable risk of fire.

ACCESS CLOSURE

Grouse shooting takes place mainly in August, September and early October. The access areas are closed on 12th August and on not more than 10 other days up to 12th December. Closure dates are published in the local press or can be had from the Head Ranger at Forton (0524) 791075. Access areas may also be closed at times of abnormally high fire risk.

DANGER WARNING

Parts of Bowland Fells were used for military training and there may still be a few unexploded bombs in some areas. If an object looks suspicious, note carefully where it is, leave it well alone and report it to a ranger or to the police as soon as possible.

BEFORE YOU SET OUT

It makes good sense to read the map and the directions to see how long it will take. How far is it? Much climbing? Rough country? Back before dark? What was the weather forecast? If you can't make it then leave enough time to get back or have a shorter alternative in mind.

DON'T INVITE TROUBLE

Bowland Fells are harmless enough on a clear sunny day but can be deceptive at times because this area of high land has a marked influence on local weather conditions. A clear day can become thick mist over the other side of the hill. Say where you are going or leave a note, it saves time if you need help.
A stout pair of shoes will be adequate for a lowland walk but on the fells, boots with ridged soles every time. Take map, compass, whistle and a small hand torch if it is likely to go dark early. If you are going on top of the fell it will be colder and perhaps windy so take waterproofs and a spare pullover. You can work up an appetite too on a walk so take enough food and drink, and for emergencies only, something concentrated like chocolate perhaps.
If you should hear it, remember that 6 blasts on a whistle or 6 flashes of a light is a distress call.

THE MAPS

The maps are based on the 1/25000 Ordnance Map and have been updated and rights of way added. The grid numbers have been omitted for simplicity but the grid corresponds with that on the Ordnance Map. 1cm on the map represents 250 metres on the ground or about 2½ inches to 1 mile. The height difference between contours is 10 metres. Close contours mean steep land.

THE DIRECTIONS

All the walks are on rights of way existing at the time of publication or on the access areas except for one or two minor deviations known to be acceptable to the farmer. The directions are generally brief enough to be remembered for the time it takes to get there. The approximate distance covered by the paragraph is given in brackets.

(Map 7) indicates the point of change to another map.

Directions are meant to be taken literally. 'Along and down' means level, then downhill. Some paragraphs give directions to something quite a long way off. This sets us off in the right direction towards something which is out of sight from the starting point. All the bearings given are magnetic bearings which are the actual readings given by the compass on the ground.

Walks requiring lengthy directions or having various starting points are divided into sections for easy reference. Where there is a choice of route a seperate section is used to describe each alternative.

> Short alternatives and minor diversions are side lined until they terminate or rejoin the main route.

THE COMPASS

A compass indicates the bearing or direction of an object. This well tried type has a circular housing in which the needle floats. It has lines on the transparent base, a numbered dial around the edge and can be rotated in relation to the base plate. *Illustration 3.*

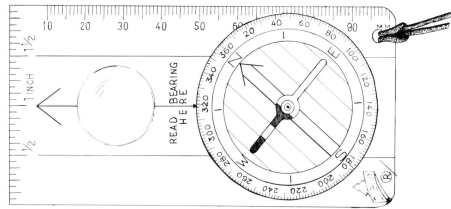

Illustration 3. The Compass.

ON THE GROUND

Face the object and hold the compass in front of you with the arrow of the base plate pointing towards the object. Keeping the baseplate steady, turn the dial until the lines in the circle are parallel to the needle. Make sure that the arrowhead in the circle is at the north end of the needle. Now read the bearing from the dial. 130° in illustration. *Illustration 4.*

ON THE MAP

To find the direction from your own position to another distant point, place the compass on the map so that the baseplate points towards the distant point, with the edge of the baseplate touching the two points on the map *Illustration 5..* Ignore the needle, but turn the dial so that the lines in the circle are parallel to the grid on the map. Make sure that the arrow in the circle points to the north end of the map. Now read the bearing. 320° in illustration.

WHICH IS NORTH

The grid lines that run towards the top of the map point to Grid North which in this area is nearly the same as True North. The compass needle always points to Magnetic North. Grid North and Magnetic North are not the same. On the ground using the compass we read magnetic bearings, and from the map we read grid bearings. Unfortunately Magnetic North varies from year to year and from place to place. The correction is applied very easily by turning the dial. In this area until 1985, Magnetic North is about 7° west of Grid North.

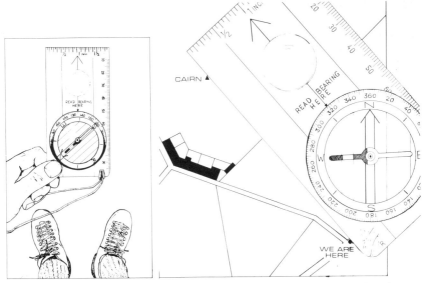

Illustration 4. Taking a bearing on the ground.   *Illustration 5. Taking a bearing from the map.*

ONE SIMPLE RULE

Where Magnetic North is west of Grid North the compass bearing is greater than the map bearing. In Bowland, bearings measured on the GROUND are GREATER by 7°. If we have measured a bearing on the map and need the equivalent value for use on the ground, we add 7 because the GROUND bearing has to be GREATER.

If we have measured a bearing on the ground and need the equivalent map bearing, we subtract 7 because the GROUND bearing was GREATER.

THE COMPASS IS NOT COMPLICATED . . .

Once you know how to measure a bearing on the ground and how to measure a bearing on the map, the rest is easy.

WALKING ALONG A BEARING . . .

To walk to something which is out of sight, measure the bearing on the map. Add 7. Hold the compass in front of you. Turn yourself until the lines in the circle are parallel to the needle with the arrowhead to the north.

Choose an object ahead which is easy to recognise, a patch of heather perhaps, and walk to it. Then with the same compass setting, pick another forward object and walk to it, and so on. Over rough peat haggs the forward object may be only 20 metres away, but in open country perhaps ½km. You may also use this method to avoid something rather that to find it, a cliff for instance.

IDENTYFING AND OBJECT . . .

To identify an object on the ground which you have seen on the map is similar to walking a bearing. Measure the bearing on the map and add 7. Hold the compass in front of you and turn round until the lines in the circle are parallel to the needle with the arrow to the north. You will now be looking towards the object but how far away you should look depends upon estimating the ground distance once you have scaled it from the map.

To identify an object on the map which you have seen on the ground, take a bearing and subtract 7. Place the compass on the map with the lines of the circle parallel to the lines of the grid and slide it along the grid line until the edge of the base plate touches your own map position. The object lies somewhere along the edge of the baseplate, but you need to estimate the distance to it. You could use the method at two different places, and see where the two lines meet.

FINDING YOUR POSITION . . .

If you are on a path but wish to know how far you are along it, identify an object on the ground, take a bearing and subtract 7. With the lines of the circle parallel to the grid, slide along the grid line until the edge of the base plate touches the object. The edge of the base plate will also cut the path at your position. The nearer the object the more reliable the result.

If you don't know where you are at all, try to identify two or three points around you on the ground. Take bearings and subtract 7 from each. Using the previous method mark the directions on the map with a pencil. They should all go through the same point and there you are.

AN OLD FRIEND . . .

The compass is extremely useful and soon becomes an old friend. But if you want the right answer, keep it away from wire fences, iron gates and that penknife in your pocket, and remember that GROUND bearings are GREATER.

If the weather gets bad or the cloud comes down, you will need your compass to get you back home, but it won't help unless you know where you are starting from. Too late to find your position when mist obscures everything. So always try to know where you are, all the time.

MAP 1 ABBEYSTEAD

This map covers the upper reaches of the Wyre. To the north the Tarnbrook Wyre rises high amongst the heather and peat of Tarnbrook Fell. It flows steeply down the fell, past the two farms and the few cottages which make up the hamlet of Tarnbrook, and then more peacefully along the road side past Lower Lee to Abbeystead. Tarnbrook is a quiet little place now but once had a thriving industry making hats.

The Marshaw Wyre has its source near the gritstone outcrop known as Millers House. The rock here was once used for making millstones and a few roughly hewn shapes still lie amongst the heather long since abandoned. Alongside the Trough road the river flows past Tower Lodge and Marshaw to join the Tarnbrook Wyre at Abbeystead Lake. This is a beautiful reach of the river, winding through the shade of mature beech and pine trees, in complete contrast to the wild open fell land just a little further up the Trough road. Below the dam at Abbeystead Lake the two rivers become the River Wyre, flowing

Photo 6. Abbeystead Lake.

through Dolphinholme and Garstang into Morecambe Bay at Fleetwood.
Most of this area belongs to the Westminster Estate centred at Abbeystead,
an attractive hamlet obviously well cared for, and set in the woodland which
surrounds the lake. Although there is no right of way around the shore, the
lake and its pair of swans perhaps, can be seen from the top of the dam. There
are plenty of well maintained public paths around Abbeystead with walks
through fields and woodland with plenty of bird life and wild flowers, whilst
Marshaw and Tarnbrook are on the edge of moorland. It is all undulating
countryside with views near and far but very little climbing.
Buses run to and from Lancaster via Dolphinholme to Abbeystead School but
the service is infrequent. There is nowhere in Abbeystead to park a car
without being in the way, but cars can be left at the bottom of Cam Brow.
This is a pleasant picnic spot by the Cam Brook on the Scorton to Trough
road.

WALK 1 (Map 1) *Cam Brow, Catshaw, Long Bridge, Abbeystead,*
            Cam Brow.
            7½ Km or 4¾ miles.
4 Km road, 1 Km firm track, 2½ Km fields. Usually dry walking. Mostly
pasture land, some woodland and a view of the lake.
By Bus: to Abbeystead School and start to walk from page 12."Abbeystead
to Cam Brow".
By Car: to Cam Brow.

CAM BROW to LONG BRIDGE.

From the top of Cam Brow the road forks to follow the wall, crosses a cattle
grid and continues to the end of the wall where we leave it to turn left along a
track (300m).
We go along the track to a gate leading to farm buildings. We go straight
through the gate with the stone building on our left and straight out onto the
lane beyond (100m).
The track goes right then left, then a long straight portion to Marl House
(500m). Here the track goes slightly right to pass the front of the house and
straight out through the gate to cross the field to another gate in a fence
(200m). We go in the same general direction parallel to the fence on our left
and soon drop down towards woodland, to a stile in the fence well to the left of
the stone wall (250m).
Over the stile a wooden footbridge, lichen encrusted, is very much safer than
it appears to be. It takes us over Cam Brook and then up a flight of steps and a
bit more to the top of a narrow embankment where we turn right (50m).
This is one side of the old mill pond and at one time there would have been
water behind this embankment which served to power the worsted mill in
Catshaw Bottom. The embankment is rather overgrown for a short distance
but is easily followed, curving left at the end to a ruined stone building which
presumably housed the mill wheel (100m).
There are several ruined buildings and a culvert which appears to have been
the tailrace for the wheel, to carry water on for use in the lower buildings.

There are channels diverting water into Cam Brook from about a four mile spread of Hawthornthwaite Fell to the south, even up as far as above Tower Lodge on the Trough road. All is now ruined almost beyond recognition though it was evidently quite a large mill in its day. The easiest way at the mill from the end of the embankment is to go straight on to the left of the first building and up the grass slope beyond it, bearing right to a small wooden gate in the fence at the top of the hill (50m).

Now straight across the field to a wooden footbridge and up steps to a small gate in the fence (100m.)

We go along with the fence on our left to the fence corner where we join up with the gravel track (150m).

> From this corner of the track the walk can be shortened by about 2 Km by turning right across the field, making towards the left hand end of the wood at the end of the old hedge (200m).
> From the gate at the corner of the wood we go steeply down the field to a footbridge over Cam Brook (250m).
> Over the footbridge and across the fence on our left, we go on to a gate in the wall near the river (50m).
> Through the gate and over the iron bridge we are on the main route again, turning right and up to the dam at the lake, *page 11* (150m).

Going straight on along the track we pass a small pond and on to Little Catshaw Farm (350m).

We go through the gate and up through another gate in the stone wall, then passing the front of the farmhouse on our right, we go straight out of the gate onto the road beyond (100m).

We bear right along the road and on to Catshaw Hall Farm (200m). The road continues to bend right as we pass a green corrugated iron shed on the right and enter the farmyard, bearing right across the yard to leave it by a wooden gate to the right of a small stone building (100m). *Photo 7.*

Keeping to the right of the hedge we go down to the wood, then left down the woodland fence to a gate (100m).

Through the gate a track goes down to a stile in the fence ahead (100m). Over

Photo 7. Catshaw Hall Farm.

Photo 8. Long Bridge over the River Wyre.

the stile into woodland the path goes down to cross a wooden footbridge over Hall Gill and on to the right along the fence side (50m). At the end of the fence we go on and bear left on level grass through trees, then sharply round to the right and down to cross the iron footbridge called Long Bridge, over the River Wyre (100m). *Photo 8.*

From Long Bridge there are two routes. Via Lentworth and the church there is some road walking. Via the lake avoids the traffic, is through fields and a little shorter.

LONG BRIDGE to ABBEYSTEAD via Lentworth.

From the bridge we go straight across to the wood, over the stile and up steps to another stile into the field (50m).

Now steeply up alongside the wood on our right until it levels out to a fence at the top (200m).

Leaving the wood we cross the stile in this fence and follow with the fence on our left to Lentworth House farm (150m).

We climb a stile on our left onto the farm road alongside the buildings, and go along the road through another gate to leave the road again by a stile on the right just before the stone wall (50m). We follow the wall on our left past a small stone building and straight on along a level grass path through crops to a stile down in the corner of the field (450m).

Over the stile and another immediately left of it we cross a footbridge and up to the church (150m).

Around to the left of the church yard wall we come to a stile on our left and a stone slab over the beck then up by the hedge to a stile at the road (300m). Turning right we keep along the road past the church drive, bending left then right to a sign post with a seat at a junction (750m). Turning right at the junction the road soon turns left and steeply down through trees to Abbeystead (700m).

LONG BRIDGE to ABBEYSTEAD via the Lake.

Across Long Bridge we turn right and follow a long pasture with Long Wood up to our left and the River Wyre a field away on our right. Further on we get closer to the river and come across a small culvert to a stile in the fence (550m).

On over the stile then up left through a gap, we come along the top side of the trees and along an old bank to a footbridge over Joshua's Beck (200m).

The path keeps up above and parallel to the river, joining the concrete road to pass the Water Authority installations, then at the bend it leaves it, crossing to the right to steps in the wall corner (300m).

Over the wall we go across grass to climb slightly to the end of the dam (100m).

The path passes the end of the dam and climbs to go through a wooden gate to a cattle grid on the road (100m).

Just beyond the next cattle grid we leave the road and cross a ditch to the right and through a gate in the stone wall (200m). Across the field towards the house in the corner we go over a white stile onto the road and turn right to Abbeystead (400m).

ABBEYSTEAD to CAM BROW.

l The bus drops down to stop at the school.
We continue on past the school, over Stoops Bridge then turn immediately
right along a road. The gate at the start of this road is usually open (200m).
(The road through gates by the lodge is private).
The river we have just crossed is the Tarnbrook Wyre and the tarred road
goes on to cross Marshaw Wyre before climbing through woodland (300m).
Both these rivers meet in the woodland about 200m to our right where they
flow into Abbeystead Lake.
Clear of the woodland the road turns right and then left before passing the
Doeholme Farm road end (400m).
Curving right at this road end, the road soon crosses a small stream and
further on another stream in the gully of Bond Clough (500m). The
farmhouse on our right is Hawthornthwaite, but we keep to the left following
the road on over the cattle grid and right to Cam Brow (500m).

WALK 2 (Map 1,2) *Tower Lodge, Tarnbrook, Abbeystead, Marshaw,*
                     Tower Lodge.
                     10½ Km or 6½ miles.
4 Kms road, 2 Km firm track, 4½ riverside paths. A varied walk, some
woodland.
By bus: to Abbeystead School starting the walk on page 14 "Abbeystead to
Tower Lodge".
By car: to Tower Lodge on the Trough Road, parking under the trees.

TOWER LODGE to TARNBROOK. (Map 2)

We start through the gate alongside Tower Lodge and up the track with the
wood on our left (300m). (Now on Map 2).
Continuing almost in a straight line along the track we pass the end of Tower
Plantation, the long wood on our right, and where the wire fence meets the
wall we go through the gate and the track fades out along level ground to
another gate in the wall (300m). Through the gate onto White Moor the path
goes left along the wall side but eventually leaves it and bears right to a sheep
fold at the wood (500m).Strictly the right of way from the end of Tower
Plantation bears left to an iron stile over the wall but the White Moor route is
easier to follow.
Through the gate by the fold, and another gate just on the right, we follow
down the wood side to stone steps in the wall corner (200m). We follow the
wall down and, skirting trees, make for the left hand gate in the fence near the
wall corner (300m).
The path keeps close to the wall on our right and then through a gate into the
yard at Spreight Clough farm buildings (100m). Down the yard and over a
small bridge the track leads through a gate and over another stone bridge then
round left towards Gilberton Farm (200m).
Just before the farm we bear right to cross Tarnbrook Wyre by a good
wooden footbridge, then on to the road at a cattle grid and along to the next
cattle grid (300m).

Just beyond the grid we meet the Tarnbrook Fell track and turn left into Tarnbrook (400m).

Through the gate we keep right to pass the farmhouse of Gornall's Farm, along the road and through a gate to Tarnbrook Cottage on our left (100m.) *Photo 9* (Map 1).

There are two ways to Abbeystead from here. The first is through fields all the way but is not easy to follow and since it goes through five hay fields we should avoid it during June and early July until the fields are mown. The other way is a quiet riverside road walk most of the way.

TARNBROOK to ABBEYSTEAD by field paths. (Map 1).

Just past Tarnbrook Cottage we go left around the wall by the tall trees and leaving the road follow the track through a gate and over Tarnbrook Wyre by a bridge, to a prominent stile alongside the gate in the wall (100m.)

We go on with the hedge on our left for a short way and then bear right to stone steps in the wall ahead near a rowan tree (100m). The next four fields are hay fields in summer. There is no path for more than a kilometer. Straight across the small field towards another small tree, over the short piece of wall, and on again in the same direction we make towards the left hand end of a dark wood in the near distance, to go over a rough stile in a short piece of wall onto a stone footbridge (150m).

The bridge brings us onto the farm track and just across slightly to the left is a narrow gap in the wall corner, and the route goes through it into the meadow (10m). *Photo 10.*

Photo 9. Tarnbrook Cottage. The field route goes left, the road to the right.

Photo 10. Crossing the farm track on the field route to Abbeystead.

We keep along the side of the meadow with the fence on our left. It soon becomes a wall and we go over a stone stile at the corner (300m). On along again with the hedge on our left, we leave it at the bend near the barn and bear over to the right towards what appears to be the right hand end of the fence by a thorn bush (300m).

Here a simple stile crosses the fence and the route is forward along the left hand side of the old hedge and ditch to a corner (100m). We leave the ditch at the corner and keep on in the same direction towards the thorn bushes just visible over the rising land ahead. Soon the roof of a farm becomes visible through the hedge ahead and we make for it, to a simple stile in a corner near the fence junction (300m).

Over the stile into another meadow we keep close around to the left to another stile in the corner (30m).

Over the stile and along towards the farm with the hedge on our right, we pass a gate and the end of an old hedge banking to join the farm road, then left to the white gate at the road (300m). At the road we cross the stile opposite in the hedge and making across the field towards the woodland we pass a fence corner and bearing left away from the fence we keep on towards the woodland to a stile in another fence (400m).

Beyond is another hay field and the path goes forward across the corner of it to keep along the edge of the woodland to a stile at the corner and straight through a short strip of garden alongside a wooden garage to the road (500m).

Bearing left we go down the road, passing the lodge at the private entrance to Abbeystead House, and just before the bridge take the road through a gate usually open on the left (400m).

TARNBROOK to ABBEYSTEAD by riverside road. (Map 1)

From Tarnbrook Cottage we follow the tarred road through the hamlet and along the river side to the few houses at the second road junction which comprise Lower Lee (2Km).

We follow the road to the right past the houses and at the first bend of the road a small gate leads to a footbridge on the left over the River Grizedale (50m). Over the bridge we go forward to join the track, passing a building and through a gate in the wall (500m).

Alongside the Tarnbrook Wyre we come to a stile onto the road (600m). We turn left over Stoops Bridge and then immediately right through the gate (50m).

ABBEYSTEAD to TOWER LODGE. (Map 1)

For those who are arriving by bus, it stops at the school and the walk starts forward along the road, over Stoops Bridge and immediately right through a gate.

Through the gate and just along this road a track goes left at the wall corner and we follow it through an iron gate into a field (100m). Bearing right we come alongside woodland to the river and cross the footbrige just before the fence surrounding the private gardens of Abbeystead House (250m).

Photo 11. Through the gate into woodland.   *Photo 12. Steps to a stone over a stream.*

Turning left along parallel to the river we pass several large clumps of woodland up on our right and then climb slightly with woodland on our left to the corner of the field with the river steeply down on our left (800m). *Photo 11.* We go through a small wooden gate into woodland then along the fence to a stile and down stone steps to a stone slab over a stream (60m). *Photo 12.* Around the bottom of the trees we go across the field towards the river again (150m).

We ignore the flat wooden footbridge down on the left and keep up along the old bank and trees to the corner of a broken wall and down to a white wooden footbridge ahead (300m).

Across the bridge and through a small wooden gate in the wall we bear right across the field keeping along the foot of the steep slope and then left along the wall and fence to come alongside the river again (200m).

We follow the fence around the end of a bank of trees into a small riverside field and across to a stile by the wood and a wooden footbridge over a stream (150m).

We follow the woodside up the hill and as it levels out to a corner, we leave it to go straight on to the left hand end of the wall ahead (250m).

We go along the side of the hedge to the corner of the field where a gate and stile lead on to the road (200m).

Onto the road at a corner we go straight on under trees, passing the road junction on our right with Well Brook Farm just below, and straight on to a bend (400m).

As the road dips, a stile on the right allows us to walk in the field away from traffic. It is not a right of way but has been made for the convenience of walkers. We follow along side the road for some distance, avoiding the temptation to rejoin the road at Marshaw Farm and keep along the field side to a stile at the wall corner by a cattle grid (600m).

The road goes by pine trees alongside the river to Tower Lodge (1½km).

Photo 13. Tarnbrook Fell from the south.

MAP 2   TARNBROOK FELL

The southern half of this map is Tarnbrook Fell. The land rises steeply from the hamlet of Tarnbrook up to the rough rocky edge of Long Crag, and then levels out onto a high plateau. Once on this flat top we are amongst a waste of gritstone outcrop, scattered heather and whinberry and peat with a little rough tussocky grass. This steep edge of the plateau cuts out all sign of habitation in the valleys to the south, and the land to the north rises steadily to a skyline of rock and peat haggs. There are no recongnisable features on this higher portion of Tarnbrook Fell and this helps to emphasise the real sense of isolation to be found on this high land. To the east is Brennand Great Hill, with further north and east, the high rocky outcrop of Wolfhole Crag. Between these at the head of Gavells Clough is another area of bare peat and sparse heather known as Woodyards on account of the old forest tree stumps which the winds and rain expose from out of the peat. This happens in other parts of the old Forest also, and much of it is birch. Once exposed to air it soon dries out and begins to deteriorate. North of the summit ridge, though it is hardly a ridge, the land drops steeply to the River Roeburn. This is Mallowdale Fell, an extensive fell from the old county boundary at the head of Whitendale along to include Mallowdale Pike, the steep sided hill with the two cairns. It looks much more of a pike when seen from the north.

The most obvious feature of Tarnbrook Fell is the gullery, about a kilometer square, above the little waterfall where the path crosses the Tarnbrook Wyre. In spring and early summer when the birds are nesting the air is full of wheeling screaming gulls in such numbers that the noise is quite deafening at times. The ground is covered with the nests of these gulls, roughly made from whatever comes readily to beak as it were. Both the eggs and the young gulls blend perfectly into the surrounding vegetation, and it is difficult to avoid treading on a nest every few paces. On the edge of this gullery I spent a pleasant 40 minutes or so in the warm spring sunshine enjoying a sandwich and a rest. As I stood up to continue my walk, I almost trod on a young gull which had been sitting motionless only a few feet from me, the whole while without my having seen it, so perfectly did it blend in with its surroundings. It is worth the climb for the gullery alone.

MAP 3 WARD'S STONE

The high land to the east of this map is Ward's Stone. It gets its name from the large boulder also called Ward's Stone at the west end of the summit plateau. This top is surprisingly flat and after a struggle through rough and often wet peat it comes as a welcome easy kilometer of level walking. At each end of the flat summit are Ordnance Survey pillars which see similar ones at Fairsnape, Ingleborough, Black Combe and Rivington.

Northwards the land slopes down to the wooded valley of Littledale, but to the west is Grit Fell and beyond it Clougha. On Grit Fell is a high cairn called Shooters Pile and southwest, past the cairn, a long straight fence goes down the hill to a small stone building with a castellated parapet by the roadside. This is Jubilee Tower built as a viewpoint in 1887 to celebrate Queen Victoria's Golden Jubilee. From here you can see the whole of Morecambe Bay and the surrounding fells.

West of the long straight fence is the access area which goes on over Clougha to the edge of Cragg Wood in Littledale. Walkers can ramble freely over this area except on a few days each year when shooting takes place. There is also an access strip which starts from the stile at the fence corner on top of Grit Fell. The strip is 12 metres wide and goes eastward over Ward's Stone then round to the south to Tarnbrook. The access strip is not a right of way, in fact there are no rights of way across these fells at all.

WALK 3 (Maps 1, 2, 3.) *Jubilee Tower, Lower Lee, Tarnbrook, Grey Crag,*
Ward's Stone, Grit Fell, Jubilee Tower.
20 km or 12½ miles.
6 km road, 3 km steep track, 11 km rough fell walking, few paths, probably
wet.

The fell portion of this walk is 11 km or 7 miles and feels like it. It is rough, some of it very much so especially if it has been wet, so it is best to realise this before setting out. The route follows the access strip along the watershed, and since there are no rights of way on these fells there is no way off the strip. It is a case of going on or going back. It is a good idea to have plenty of time for this walk because there are areas of peat haggs which make the going awkward and time consuming.

A compass is essential, especially in poor weather conditions.

By car: to Jubilee Tower Car Park, Photo 14.

By parking the car here we can walk the road portion first rather than be faced with it after a long fell walk. We set off towards the Trough past the road end which is signposted to Abbeystead and on to a cattle grid (2km).

The road goes steeply down through trees to level out across the River Grizedale to a group of houses which comprise Lower Lee (1½km)(Map 1). Along to the left here it is a riverside walk by the Tarnbrook Wyre to the hamlet of Tarnbrook (2km).

The road through the hamlet passes the first farm house on the left and then a cottage on the right before going through a gate (200m).

The road passes a cottage garden and another farmhouse on the left, and beyond on the left is a gravel track through a gate onto open fell (100m).

The gate has a sign reading 'Gilberton'. The track goes on with a fork to a cattle grid, but we keep left along the track and left also at the next fork (800m).(Map 2).

The track climbs steadily and steeply up the side of Tarnbrook Fell. It eventually becomes a path past an open fronted shelter, then crosses Tarnbrook Wyre above a small waterfall (2km). From the waterfall the route crosses the gullery where in the spring and early summer the air is full of gulls. The route is waymarked by posts and an occasional cairn but is not very easy to find without care. It is advisable to use the compass if there is any doubt. The route goes up over heather and peat to the flat top (1km).

At the top the surface becomes mostly bare peat over a large area. In dry weather it is dusty and finds its way into boots, eyes and sandwiches. We turn left across this peat to a stone wall (600m).

We go along with the wall on our right, turning left at the corner (300m).

Then following wall, fence, or remains of it, then wall to Grey Crag (1km). This is a large boulder over the wall to the north. It is not what one expects a crag to be. Its smaller neighbour to the south of the wall is a much more interesting creature. We follow the wall to leave it at the corner (500m). Turning left here we follow the waymarkers across open rough fell to the col (500m).

Photo 14. Jubilee Tower.   *Photo 15. Queen's Chair.*

Then comes a steep rise to the top of Ward's Stone (500m). Near the top is Queen's Chair, a natural rock outcrop, *Photo 15,* quite small about the size and shape of a stool.

At the top of the rise is another natural rock feature called Grey Mare and Foal. The foal is fairly evident but the mare requires a bit of imagination. A short way north west of this rock is the Ordnance Survey pillar, and it is level easy walking across the flat top of the fell to the second pillar (700m). (Map 3). Near the westerly pillar is the tall outcrop of Ward's Stone which probably signifies its status as a boundary mark, and gives its name to this high portion of fell land. The path now goes steeply down amongst rock and then levels out across heather and peat to cross a track (2km). This track is a private shooting track and eventually leads south down to Higher Lee. It is private, and the access strip crosses it, and soon rises to the cairns at the top of Grit Fell and the fence corner (1km).

At the corner is a stile which we cross. Straight on along the fence is the stile which leads on to Clougha, but we turn left over the stile and follow the fence downhill past the tall cairn known as Shooters Pile. This fenced area of fell land is Hare Appletree Fell. The fence side is a little bit marshy halfway down and in wet weather may require a detour. Close to the bottom, the path leaves the fence to cross Worm Syke to the right hand corner of the car park (2km).

Photo 16. Clougha Pike.

MAP 4 CLOUGHA

Pronounced Cloffa which is a little confusing because most of the fellside
valleys are called Cloughs pronounced Cloo. Some of these valleys are quite
deep, others fairly shallow. Some have a stream in the bottom whilst others
are dry but they are all cloughs. The name is used in other parts of the north
of England, but the pronunciation 'cloo' is probably local to Bowland. The
Bowland fells are also something of a watershed for names. Mostly they are
Becks to the north and Brooks to the south.

Clougha is a rough rocky fell, though it is much more accessible than it
appears to be when seen from the Rigg Lane car park at Quernmore. This
northwest corner is a steep mass of loose rocks and outcrop with hardly any
vegetation at all, but this is only the lower slope, above it is still rather rocky
but reasonable walking. To the south it is rough grassland and can be rather
wet in parts. To the north it is deep in heather, whinberry and boulders, rather
steep but drier.

The west slope rises to a steep rocky edge called Clougha Pike where a large
cairn and two rough circular shelters jostle the OS pillar for the best position
on this locally high point. Eastward the land rises to the top of Grit Fell, with
its high cairn called Shooters Pile, and just below it the ancient boundary
stone of 1692 marking the extent of Hare Appletree Fell which slopes down

to and across the main road. Here near its southern extent is Jubilee Tower built as a viewpoint though much the same view can be had from the road, and another car park. There is a third car park north of Clougha on the Littledale Road at Little Cragg.

These three car parks serve the main access area which extends from Jubilee Tower to the edge of Cragg Wood at Littledale. There are also two small access areas here. Little Cragg which adjoins the car park south of the unfenced road, and Baines Cragg, a small rocky ridge just to the west alongside unfenced road.

The Access Areas are all privately owned but agreements have been reached to allow public access on all but a few days a year, subject to the byelaws displayed. Dogs are not allowed since this is sheep and grouse country, and fires and stoves must not be lit so as to avoid peat fires which can burn for months.

Since this is an area for rambling about, directions are also given for the easiest routes to the top from each car park and for those who wish to go up and down by different routes, the distances back around the road.

The route to the top from Quernmore Post Office is a right of way.

The distances by road around the main access points and the car parks are given in miles and kilometres. The distances are all from the start so the total distance round is 4¾ miles.

Kms.	Mls.			Kms	Mls.
0	0	Jubilee Tower Car Park	Little Cragg Car Park	0	0
1½	1	Cattle Grid	Far corner of Cragg Wood	1	½
3	2	Quernmore Post Office turn right at cross roads	Turn left at cross roads into Rigg Lane	1¾	1
3½	2½	Fork right into Rigg Lane	Rigg Lane Car Park Quernmore	3	1¾
4½	3	Rigg Lane Car Park Quernmore	Keep left at road junction	4	2¼
5¾	3¾	Turn right at cross roads into Littledale Road	Qernmore Post Office turn left at cross roads	4½	2¾
6½	4¼	Near corner of Cragg Wood.	Cattle grid	6	3¾
7½	4¾	Little Crag Car Park	Jubilee Tower Car Park	7½	4¾

The routes up and down are not greatly different in length. In order of difficulty, with the easiest first they are:-

Quernmore Post Office ... Easy but no car park and little roadside parking.

Rigg Lane Car Park ... fairly good walking but rather steep in places

Jubilee Tower Car Park ... fairly good walking but rather longer

Little Cragg Car Park ... rough in parts and requires a compass

UP from JUBILEE TOWER CAR PARK 3km or 2 miles.

From the back corner of the car park we cross Worm Syke and steadily up alongside the fence past Shooters Pile to the corner (2km).

The access strip joins in here at a stile but we turn left to the stile at the next corner (200m).

There is a fairly clear waymarked path continuing in the same general direction through heather to the 3 Chairs Cairn which is prominently placed on a rock outcrop. (500m).

UP from QUERNMORE POST OFFICE. 3km or 2 miles.

Up the road from the corner of the post office the road bends left then sharp right at white iron railings (300m).

We turn left here over a cattle grid and up a tarred road to the top of the field (400m).

Over the cattle grid on the left we go past a few houses in trees. There is a sign near the cattle grid indicating straight on to Clougha which is correct but our route is simpler, also a right of way, and keeps to the left hand route. We follow the road over the beck and go on up to the next cattle grid (200m).

Bending right, the road goes up to the farm gateway (200m).

We go straight up the farmyard and then through the right hand gate at the wall corner (70m).

The track bends right over the beck and left again along the wall (150m).

We follow the track straight on past the corner of the wall keeping on parallel and close to the clough and through a gate in the fence (200m).

Then alongside the wooded clough to the wall ahead (200m).

We go through the left hand gate and along a narrow strip of field alongside the clough edge and out through another gate (200m).

Then parallel to the beck out through the gate in the last wall (200m).

The path is a bit vague but keeps parallel to the beck until just beyond an old sheepfold at a wall end down on the left (200m).

We bend left to cross the beck upstream of the sheepfold and follow parallel to the wall to come steeply to the pillar (450m).

UP from RIGG LANE CAR PARK. 3km or 2 miles

From the back of the car park, over the stile by the gate, we follow a good track leaving it at the corner to go to the right down a rougher track and right again towards an iron gate (250m).

Over the stile to the left of the gate we go over duck boards alongside the wall to the next stile (150m).

Following the wall again, we leave it near a stone culvert to go through gorse and past the other end of the stone culvert on our right (150m).

A reasonable path goes through some small saplings, then a few more oak saplings, keeping left and up, with the beck and the wall down on our right, to stiles at the wall corner *Photo 17* (350m).

Photo 17. Stiles at the wall corner.   *Photo 18. Left around the rock outcrop.*

There are two ways from here. The first up Windy Clough is rather difficult.
Over the left stile and straight on along the valley side we drop down to the valley bottom beyond a few trees (100m).
Keeping in the valley bottom all the way there is no path but reasonable walking for a while, then it gets more difficult through rocks to the wall (350m).
Over the stile we turn right and very steeply up alongside the wall, more of a scramble than a walk (150m).
Once up this rough bit it is better to keep a little way out from the wall to avoid three similar but smaller cloughs, to come over a stile to the left of the first angle of the wall (400m).
The easier route avoids Windy Clough and is shorter.
Over the left stile we turn sharp right and follow the long straight wall steeply to the top corner (200m).
We continue in the same direction beyond the wall corner (118°) climbing a little to come in sight of a rock outcrop on the near skyline. Making for the high point of the outcrop we shall find as we get nearer that there are actually two. Climbing up to the left of the lower outcrop we keep along its top edge on a flat shelf of heather to avoid most of the rock then left around the upper outcrop towards the wall at the stile (300m).
From the stile the wall climbs steadily up towards the rocky edge of Clougha Pike and we follow it with the wall on our left to its end (500m).
Here we climb a few rocks round the end of the wall and leaving the fence to our left, follow the top edge of the outcrop to the pillar (400m).

WALK 4 (Map 4)   *Little Cragg Car Park, Clougha Pike, Rigg Lane, Little Cragg. 9kms or 5½ miles.*

1Km road with little traffic, 1km firm tracks, 1km field paths, 6kms fell walking, some of it rough with no paths in parts.

Clougha is not particularly steep, but the routes are not very conspicious and there are few landmarks, so it is an area where it is easy to get lost. A compass is essential.

By car: to Little Cragg Car Park or to Rigg Lane Car Park and start the walk on page 26 "Rigg Lane Car Park to Little Cragg Car Park".

UP from LITTLE CRAGG CAR PARK

We set off along the road to the gate on the right before the cattle grid (150m). Then follow the vague track down the field keeping to the right of a small stone building at the wall junction (150m).

From here the route is waymarked with yellow arrows. We follow the wall down and round to the left on a track to the bottom (250m).

Forward through the second gateway the track goes along the wall by two thorn trees towards Skelbow Barn (200m).

We keep left of the barn through a gateway, along a track between hedge and wall, then turn right at the wall corner to follow the red arrow up a grass track to a gate (200m).

The path goes along past a tree to a stile in the wall (120m).

We turn right over the stile and left just before the beck. It can be wet at times near the wall (40m).

A track wends its way up alongside the beck which is the River Conder and levels and fades out towards a wall corner with an old sheepfold (300m).

> Going direct to the pillar from here is very rough in deep heather with hidden boulders and hidden gaps between them, but for those who wish to try it, a bearing of 215° from the wall corner leads to a cairn on one of the many small quarry holes (700m).
>
> Then on again along the same bearing to the fence (700m).
>
> Across the fence and on the same bearing again to the pillar (200m).

The path we take is via the Three Chairs Cairn which although easier walking does require care with the compass and it is important to keep a note of where we are along the path because it fades out near the top. The cairn mentioned on the direct route appears as a tall thin cairn on the skyline and this can be useful for a compass check of our position along the path.

About 30m before the sheepfold at the wall corner, two small cairns (180°) indicate the direction of the route but there is no path just yet (120m). From here the path bears left and improves, following the lower edge of the heather with bracken on our left. The firm path fades out at the top of the brow (200m).

It is important to find the Access Area marker post which is on a bearing of 168° (200m). We can either go direct to it or keep along the vague path and bear right and the path becomes more definite.

From the post 161° is a stone grouse butt (130m).
Then a good hollow path past 3 more grouse butts (120m).
From the last grouse butt the path is fairly obvious but not well marked (155°) until it becomes a distinct hollow path again (130m).
The hollow path is well defined up over the skyline to another stone grouse butt (150m).
Hollow path again (215°) to another stone grousebutt (70m).
The hollow path continues (195°) over the skyline to a flat extent of heather where the path turns right and fades (90m).
From the corner at the end of the hollow path 216° there is another Access Area marker post (50m) and the vague path bends round to it.
From the post 2 small cairns mark the limit of access but the direction of the Three Chairs cairn is slightly right (214°) on a small lump on the skyline. There is no path from here and it is important to keep carefully along the bearing because the bump on the skyline becomes less conspicuous the nearer we get to it and finally disappears from view. Following this bearing we pass to the right of a large chunky rock outcrop (200m).
Then on again to the cairn (300m).
The Three Chairs cairn is built on a small shelf of rock and somewhat elevated and it would be a good idea to enlarge it so that it is readily recognisable from the other cairns which waymark the ridge route. From the cairn the path is fairly distinct with waymarker cairns. We follow the path to the west and it becomes more rocky and dips down to a stile at the wire fence (400m).
Keeping up on the top from here it is fairly level to the pillar (300m).

DOWN to RIGG LANE CAR PARK

This is Clougha Pike and we go north along the top edge of the rocky outcrop to meet the fence and follow it down to the start of the wall (400m).
Climbing down a few rocks around the start of the wall we follow it down with the wall on our right to the stile which is just beyond the angle of the wall (500m).

We keep to the near side of the wall and beyond the stile go down to the left (225°) around the bottom of the rock outcrop *Photo 18* (100m).
Keeping on the flat heather along the top of the lower rock outcrop, we pass to the right of a large boulder down to the wall corner (298°) (200m).
Keeping the wall on our left we follow it steeply down to a stile at the wall junction (200m).
Over the stile we follow the lower path and keeping right of a few oak saplings, pass a stone culvert on our left, then through gorse to pass the other end of the culvert and along the wall side to a stile (350m).
Over the stile we follow the wall on duckboards across wet land and over a stile onto the track (150m).
Turning right up the track leads on to Little Cragg but for the car park we leave it to fork left around the shoulder of the fell and left again down to the stile at the car park (250m).

RIGG LANE CAR PARK to LITTLE CRAGG CAR PARK

From the stile at the back of the car park a good firm track goes up and bears left to join a similar track (150m).

From here the track is more or less level and generally in the same direction for 1km. We keep left at a cairn (700m).

About 50m further on is a stone pillar then level along to a substantial aqueduct bridge (350m).

Over the bridge we keep straight on coming closer to the wall on our left. The wall steps to the right then on again and just beyond is a gate and stile (300m).

Over the stile we go down the field, across the beck and keep to the right of the house up the track to the main road. (300m).

We turn right alongside Cragg Wood and over the cattle grid to the car park (1km). Those who started from Rigg Lane should now continue from the start of the walk on page 24 "Up from Little Cragg Car Park".

DOWN to JUBILEE TOWER CAR PARK 3kms or 2 miles.

From the Three Chairs cairn the route goes easterly and is waymarked with small cairns. It makes up towards the stile at the end of the fence (600m).

Over the stile the route is straight on towards the large cairn called Shooters Pile. (300m).

From here it follows the long straight fence down to the car park (2kms).

DOWN to QUERNMORE POST OFFICE 3kms or 2 miles

Standing at the pillar on Clougha Pike and looking down over the scar towards Quernmore we can see most of the route down, but the start is unexpectedly behind us to our left and goes around the back of the shelter (165°) steeply down through rocks on a rough path (100m).

Less steeply down and bearing right the vague path is parallel to the wall on our right, crosses a small beck, then bends right parallel to it to go through a gate in the wall ahead (550m).

Keeping close to the beck we go through the right hand of two gates in the wall ahead, along a narrow strip of field to a gate in the wall, then on alongside the wooded clough to a gate in the fence (600m).

On in the same direction is a wall corner and a good track goes round to the right, over the beck and left into the farmyard through a gate (350m).

Straight on down the farmyard we go out onto a tarred road alongside some large modern buildings and straight on down over a cattle grid (270m).

The road crosses a beck in trees and on to another cattle grid (200m).

On down we meet the main road at another cattle grid (400m).

Down again round two bends to the post office at the crossroads (300m).

DOWN to LITTLE CRAGG CAR PARK 3km or 2 miles

From the Three Chairs cairn there is no path for a while and a compass bearing of 34° must be followed carefully to find an Access Area marker post at the start of the path. We pass a large rock outcrop on our right (300m).

On the same bearing it is fairly level through heather to the post (200m).

From the post on a bearing of 36° it is 50m to the start of a distinct hollow path. The path from the post appears to be going the wrong way but bends round to the start of the path proper (50m).

It is a good hollow path past two grouse butts (300m).

Then the path becomes less distinct to a stone grouse butt (130m).

A good hollow path again now past 3 more grouse butts to an Access Area marker post (250m).

From the post a bearing of 348° brings us to the start of a good path (200m). At the bottom the path bears right and fades out towards the wall corner and an old sheepfold (320m).

Here we bear left past a cairn to meet an old grass track which follows the top of the clough and wends its way down towards an iron gate in the wall, but we keep along to the right to a stile near the wall corner (250m).

Over the stile and past a tree, we go through a gate and down a grass track, turning left at the bottom to Skelbow Barn. (320m).

From here the route is waymarked by yellow arrows and keeps right of the barn, comes alongside the wall and left through a gate (200m).

Up past a thorn tree the track goes round the wall corner, past a small building on the right then forward to a gate onto the road near the cattle grid and left to the car park (550m).

Photo 19. Riverside Pasture in Roeburndale.

MAP 5 ROEBURNDALE

The old and beautiful little village of Wray is at the meeting of the Rivers Roeburn and Hindburn. Here are hotels, the village shop and post office and 17th century houses sturdily built in stone. Down the hill to the stone bridge are roadside cottages with flowers at the door and cobbled pavements.

From the bridge a road leads out of Stauvin and Harterbeck which is Roeburndale East. Higher up the village, the road alongside the post office goes to Roeburndale West, which extends from Whit Moor Gate to Haylots, Mallowdale and up beyond High Salter.

Much of Roeburndale is open moorland but the River Roeburn is attractively wooded. Near Barkin Bridge is a cool spot for a bathe on a hot summer day, the deep pool shaded by overhanging trees and steep rock. The woodland is beautiful in Spring and the russet and gold of autumn well worth a visit. Downstream of the bridge, Roeburndale is a steep rocky valley almost entirely wooded but with a few secluded fields by the river. It is a pity that there is no right of way along the valley. It would be a particularly attractive walk with woodland and riverside cliffs, and plenty of wild flowers and birds. Without a path it is difficult and after rain it can be dangerous too. There is a right of way to the river from both sides but it is rather meaningless because there is no longer any bridge. The path crossed the river at Backsbottom Farm but both the farm and its bridge were destroyed in a disastrous flood.

The storm of 8th August 1967 is vividly remembered by everyone who experienced it. There were narrow escapes as the flood water swept all before it, destroying bridges and washing away cottages in the village as it poured across the road into the Lune Valley. The little roadside garden where the cottages once stood is the only visible reminder of the disaster which struck this quiet little village.

The bus from Lancaster to Bentham goes through the village. The train goes through Wennington 3 kms away.

WALK 5 (Map 5)   *Wray, Harterbeck, Low Salter, Wray, or Hornby.*
                        11 km or 7 miles.
7 km road with little traffic, 4 km field paths. Generally dry easy walking, some woodland and river.
By train: to Wennington and walk to Wray 3 kms.
By bus: to Wray from Lancaster or Bentham.
By car: to Wray. There is little parking in the village, but space for a few cars just after the start of the walk over the bridge and sharp back round to the right to a layby at the first bend above the river side. There is much more parking space at the crossroads 2 km nearer Lancaster which adds 2 km to the start of the walk but is convenient for the finish if we take the Hornby road back again.

WRAY to HARTERBECK

We leave the village of Wray by the stone bridge at the east end of the village
and turn sharp right to double back along the other side of the river. There are
a few houses and the road begins to climb past the drive to the reservoir on the
right, then Alcocks Farm also on the right (1km), (Map 5).

A haytime diversion for June and early July continues along the road to a
cross roads where we turn right to a cattle grid (1km).

We cross the grid and leaving the road turn left along the wall side, then
between walls and out through a gate 300m).

Or we could avoid most of the field paths by keeping to the main road.

The road crosses two cattle grids, left around Stauvin Farm, over another
grid and on to Harterbeck (3kms).

Entering Harterbeck farmyard at the road end we go sharp left through a
gate at the end of the long building (20m). *Photo 20.*

At other times we can take the field route.

Beyond Alcocks Farm on the right a gate opens into a small field (500m).
We keep left across the field to find a stile in a short piece of wall by a thorn
bush (30m).

Through the stile we follow up the hedge on our right towards the top of
the field where the barn is on the skyline, over rails in the hedge ahead and
on in the same direction to meet the farm road at a cattle grid (600m).
Care is needed here to avoid losing the way. As we approach the grid a
wall goes on in the same direction beyond the grid. We follow this wall
keeping it on our left hand side, then going between walls for a short way
we go out through a gate (300m).

Photo 20. Harterbeck Farm.

We keep the wall on our left, through a gate in the wall ahead, then through a small gate in the next wall just beyond the power line (700m).

We follow the broken wall in the same general direction, over a poor stile in the wall ahead and on again along the broken wall past a small thorn tree (400m).

Through a gap in the wall ahead and over a stone culvert we follow the ditch along towards a tree to go over a rather better stile in the wall. Beyond is a hay field so we keep around the edge of the field, passing the rowan tree and round the bend to go through a gate to the right of the barn (200m).

On a firm track we go up with the wall on our left. The track passes two gates on the left and then goes through a gate in the wall ahead and left up to Harterbeck Farm (600m).

At the end of the track we enter the farm through a gate, keeping straight on with the farm buildings on our left and the wall on our right. We turn left at the open fronted building and follow the long building to the far end, then right, through a gate at the corner of the building (70m). *Photo 20*

HARTEBECK to LOW SALTER

From the corner of the building the track fords a beck but there is a stone slab for walkers alongside the wall. The track curves away from the wall but we go down to the bend of the wall and then left by a definite path to cross Goodber Beck above the waterfall (300m).

There is no path from here. We leave the beck and go steeply up the hill to join the fence on our left, soon leaving it again to follow around the top of the steep land to our right. Near a thorn bush the route bears left to follow the power line to a gate in the wall (400m).

Through the gate we go along the track with the wall on our right. It soon becomes a fence and we go through a gate and forward again to come alongside the fence with the bushes in it over to our right, and on towards Low Salter Farm (500m).

Near the farm the track goes through a gate on our right which brings us into a narrow walled strip of field which leads down to the farmyard. We go straight on keeping the main farm buildings on our left and out to the road at the Methodist Church (200m).

LOW SALTER to WRAY

Down the road from the Methodist Church we come to Barkin Bridge (300m). The picturesque bends of the River Roeburn on the right are often explored but there is no right of way off the road. Up the steep hill and past the buildings the road crosses a cattle grid onto Whit Moor (1km).

We leave the moor at another cattle grid known as Whit Moor Gate and go down to a fork in the road (1km).

Left goes to Hornby (2km).

Right goes to Wray (1½km).

Photo 21. Barkin Bridge over the River Roeburn.

WALK 6 (Map 5)   *Barkin Bridge, Haylots, Mallowdale, Salter, Barkin Bridge 5km or 3 miles.*
4km road, 1km field & woodland paths. Generally dry easy walking.
By car: Take the Roeburndale West road from Hornby or Wray, over Whit Moor and drop steeply to cross Warm Beck and River Roeburn at Barkin Bridge Photo 21. Park either side of the bridges.

We walk south up the hill and at a bend just beyond the Methodist Church we go through a gate on the right (400m).
Down the tarred road we cross the River Roeburn at a culvert replacing the old Drunken Bridge just downstream (400m).
When the river is high the culvert becomes a ford, in which case it will be difficult to cross Mallowdale Gill upsteam and we would be wise to turn back. Over the culvert we go up to Haylots (700m).
The road goes on through a gate but just before it we leave the road through another gate on the left at a stone building. It leads into a small field and we go left through a gate to the bottom right hand corner of a narrow field and a stile in the wall (200m).
Over the stile the path follows the edge of the woodland to enter it at a simple stile (150m), *Photo 22*

A grass path through the wood meets the stream at a peice of flat rock where we cross and over the fence by a rough stile (150m).

We follow the fence upstream for a short way and just before the wire fence we turn steeply up the slope to the farmhouse (200m).

This is Mallowdale and we go through a small fenced yard, through a gate between the buildings, past the front of the farmhouse and straight down the farm road (50m).

Steeply down to Mallowdale bridge and over two cattle grids we come up to the road (1km).

Left over the cattle grid we go down past Middle Salter and the Methodist Church to Barkin Bridge (1km).

Photo 22. Across Mallowdale Gill towards Mallowdale Farm.

WALK 7 (Map 5)   Barkin Bridge, Salter, Mallowdale, Haylots, Winder, Thornbush, Barkin Bridge. 7km or 4½ miles.

4km road, 3km paths. Generally dry, may be muddy at Winder.
By car: Take the Roeburndale West road from Hornby or Wray, over Whit Moor and drop steeply to cross Warm Beck and River Roeburn at Barkin Bridge. Photo 21. Park either side of the bridges.

We walk south up past the Methodist Church and Middle Salter then turn right at a cattle grid by a stone barn (1km).

HIGH SALTER BARN to ROEBURNDALE ROAD.

Down over two cattle grids we cross River Roeburn and come steeply up to Mallowdale Farm (1km).

Past the front of the farmhouse we go through a small gate at the far end of the house and through a small fenced yard (50m).

There is no path across the field but we make westerly to the wood. Across the valley there are several groups of buildings. We make towards the group furthest to the left which brings us towards a large sycamore tree and around the end of a group of trees (200m).

We must be sure to set off correctly or we shall miss the bridge, if it has been erected again after the last flood. To the right down the fence a few metres a rough stile leads to a rocky part of the stream which we cross to a well made grass path (50m).

Crossing the beck after heavy rain needs care but is usually easy. The path climbs to the right and leaves the wood at a simple stile where we turn right along the edge of the wood to a stone stile at the end of the wall (300m).

Over the stile we go left up a narrow field, through a gate in the wall at the top, then right through another gate onto the road near a stone building near Haylots Farm (200m).

We follow the tarred road through the gate then right, on and down across the beck, then up to the gate onto Roeburndale Road (1km).

ROEBURNDALE ROAD to BARKIN BRIDGE

We turn right along the tarred road to Winder Farm (200m).

Keeping up to the left of the farmyard along the track, we pass a stone building on our right, and on along the track pass the next stone building Hill Barn (250m).

The track bears slightly left at the barn and follows a wall to a gate at a small conifer plantation (100m).

The track goes straight on with the wall on our right. It fades out and it is easier to cross through a gap and keep the wall on our left (150m).

The wall ends and we follow a ditch on our left to an iron gate at a fence corner (200m).

There is no path here for about a kilometre and the route is not easy to find. Through the gate we bear away from the fence on our left (30°) over a slight rise to pass a flat heap of stones on our left, and on to the left hand end of the woodland in Warm Beck Gill (250m).

There is a small waterfall at this last tree, but before we get down to it we bear left to pass two small thorn bushes to avoid a marshy area. We cross the beck to the left of the bare earth slopes ahead (50m).

Across the beck the route is steeply up a hollow to cross the wall by a stone stile (50m).

The stile is hard to find, but it is just left of an old gateway which has been built across with stone walling. The stile is rather awkward to get over. Over the wall we go straight up away from the wall and over the brow (40°) to come alongside a fence on our right into a corner where three fences meet (400m).

Two rails in the right hand fence serve as a stile, and over it we follow with the fence on our left through an iron gate and down the strip of conifer trees to a track (300m).

We go along the track to Thornbush farm, following the track round to the right at the near end of the buildings. Keeping the buildings on our left we go along the yard and out down the track to the road (400m).

Turning right at the road we cross the cattle grid and on past a stone building, steeply down to Barkin Bridge. (1km).

Photo 23. River Roeburn flowing by Cowfold Scar.

Photo 24. The Great Stone of Fourstones.

MAP 6 LOWGILL

The road from Slaidburn wends its way down from Cross of Greet, a quiet road over open moorland with lapwing and curlew and views to Ingleborough and the Fells of Furness. Across Tatham Fells the road goes on towards Bentham past the Great Stone of Fourstones. This great boulder is on the county boundary. North of here is Yorkshire.

The old Roman Road was further west. It came down Bottom Head Fell and along the side of the valley. It is more obvious from a distance than close at hand, but it can be seen well enough as a wide slightly raised embankment where it crosses open fields. The little hamlet of Lowgill is on the Roman Road, just a few houses, the church and school and a telephone box. It did once have a pub but not nowadays.

The valley of the Hindburn is pleasantly wooded. There are quiet lanes, good walks through fields and by the river, with primroses and bluebells in the woods.

There is a local school bus from Hornby, but otherwise Lowgill is a little way from public transport. It is about 3km or 2 miles from bus or train. Some buses between Wray and Bentham go via Millhouses and stop at the Lowgill road end. That is the name of the bus stop to ask for, or alternatively go on into Bentham. The distance is much the same either way. From the Lowgill road end bus stop the road goes eastwards for about 5kms to meet the Slaidburn to Bentham road where there is a convenient layby for cars. The walks in this area start either from the layby or from the lane to church about 2km west of it.

Bus to Lowgill Road End. Between Millhouses and Bentham.
We leave the bus route and walk towards Lowgill passing a road end on our left and another on our right, then along with the wood on our right to a crossroads with a signpost (2km).
The Lowgill road bears down to the right, but we take the quieter road straight on past the post towards Slaidburn. The first road on the right is a narrow lane signposted 'To the Church' (1km).
Bus or Train to Bentham. The bus stops at the Brown Cow Hotel and immediately opposite is the road to the station (250m).
From the station we go down to the River Wenning, then straight up the hill, passing a terrace of stone houses at a bend, to the crossroads at Mewith Lane 1½km.
Straight on up again the road comes onto open fell at a cattle grid, past a farm road end, and straight on up past the Great Stone of Fourstones to the first road junction on the right. It has a signpost. (1½km).
Just along the side road is a layby (100m).
By car The easiest approach is from the Bentham to Slaidburn road over Tatham Fells.
By Car from Slaidburn. From Cross of Greet we pass the Botton signpost and sheepfolds in a dip of the road keeping straight on, then dropping steeply around bends to cross Crossdale Beck and up again onto open fell at a cattle grid, for 1km to the second of two close road ends where we turn left to a layby just along on the left.
By Car from Bentham. Onto open fell at a cattle grid it is 1km to the first road end just past the Great Stone of Fourstones. We turn right here to a layby just along on the left of the road.

WALK 8 (Map 6)   *Church, Botton Mill, Botton Head, Lowgill or Ringstones 15km or 9 miles.*
10km road, 1km firm track, 4km field paths generally dry.

From the LAYBY
By the left fork over the cattle grid we leave open fell along the walled road to the second lane on the left signed 'To the Church' (2km).

From CHURCH LANE to BOTTON MILL
Along the lane we pass the gates of the Church of the Good Shepherd and by steep sharp bends down to the Lowgill Road (1km).
We turn left, round over the bridge and up to the corner (200m).
Through the gate at the corner we make for the tallest tree. Keeping above the woodland through a gate we join a track on the left, go through a gate by the stone barn and down to the wood (500m).
As the track turns at the wood we leave it and go over a stile to steps through the wood and forward to cross the River Hindburn at the footbridge (150m).
Round to the left and up, the path enters woodland and goes up through bluebells to a stone stile into the field corner (150m).
We continue uphill keeping the wooded stream on our right. If it is haytime and the grass is long it is better to keep straight on for a little way beyond the end of

Photo 25. Across a stream to a short deep clough.   *Photo 26. Past electricity poles to the footbridge.*

the trees to where the grass is shorter along the route of an old track which goes across left to a stone barn (300m).

At other times we can go direct from the end of the wood to the barn. There is no marked track for some way yet. We go through the gate at the stone building, across through the next gate by the tallest tree, then straight again keeping left of the barn and through the gate (300m).

We follow the power line through a few trees and then go down a short deep clough to a gate (100m) *Photo 25.*

We may see the red squirrel about the trees near this gate. Through the gate the path soon becomes more obvious. If follows the trace of an old wall across a small beck and past the front of an old barn (200m).

The track is clear as it climbs slightly, then drops slightly left but still on high ground, goes through the gap in the old wall down to river level and through the gate at the fence (300m).

We keep along the riverside to the road corner and turn right (400m).

A change of scene here as a small tributary of the Hindburn flows through a damp oak wood with a flora of Liverwort, Hairy Woodrush, Celandine, Primroses, Ramsons, Moschatel and Wood Anemones. We go up the road with the stream on our left, round to the left at the road junction and past the cottage which used to be Botton Mill with its little waterfall (500m).

BOTTON MILL to WHITRAY

The fenced road passes a barn on the right and Lower Thrushgill farm which is down to our left, and then there is a short piece of unfenced road to a sharp corner where the road goes on to Higher Thrushgill. We leave the road at this corner (1km).

The line of the Roman Road is quite plain across the valley but much harder to find when it is close at hand. From the road corner a rough track leads down through a gate and bends down to Botton Bridge. Over the bridge and up the fence side we come to another gate at the top (500m).

Through the gate we keep up the hedge side along a firm track which soon leaves the hedge and crosses over the field to Botton Head Farm (500m). This is a hay field. The track comes into the farmyard by a gate and we turn immediately left through another gate onto the road again. Round the bend through a gate we cross Middle Gill, then with the wall on our left go along to a sharp corner and Whitray Farm on the left (500m).

WHITRAY to LAYBY and BENTHAM

Shorter by a kilometre, an alternative road walk back to the layby or Bentham goes past the farm gate, down over Whitray Beck with its grove of conifers and up to meet the Lythe Fell road (1km).

We turn left over Green Syke Bridge by the sheepfolds, on over the cattle grid and straight up to the right of the signpost to the next cattle grid by the stone building (1km).

Now at first between fences we go down over Balshaw Bridge and up again onto open fell at the next cattle grid (1km).

Along to the second road on the left (1km).

Left is the layby, or straight on for Bentham

WHITRAY to IVAH

Just before the corner we turn in at Whitray Farm gate and keep straight through between farm buildings on both sides and along a straight track between walls (200m).

The track opens into a field and the route is straight on, at first with a wall on the left, then across open field to a footbridge over Whitray Beck (500m).

Before dropping down to the bridge, notice across the valley an old stone barn partly in ruins. If we make generally in this direction it is obvious which bridge to cross. Straight across the bridge in the hedge opposite is a stile gap in a short portion of wall. We go through the stile and steeply up the field ahead. Shortly the old barn will be visible (200m).

There is no path for a while yet, but the compass bearing from the stile is 320°. Keeping the barn is sight on our right hand we make across more level ground over a small ditch and on to a gate in a rather low stone wall (200m). We go on in much the same direction straight across a short stretch of field to a little gate and a culvert over Williamson's Gill then with the hedge on our left we go on to 'Swans' (500m).

The path leads through gates between the house and the old farm buildings onto a gravel road and down to the tarred road where we go round the corner to the right and up to Ivah Farm (700m).

There are two routes from here. The first is more convenient for the Millhouses bus route and the second is more convenient for Bentham.

For MILLHOUSES

We turn left through Lowgill, on past the school then round and down to
Crossdale Beck (1km).
Over the bridge then right through a gateway between the old building and the
cottage and up around sharp bends past the church gates to the lane end
(700m).
The Lowgill Road End bus stop is to the left (3km).
To the right along and over the cattle grid is the layby (2km).
Beyond it and left is the road to Bentham.

For BENTHAM

We turn right and up to the junction at the top then left along Craggs Lane
(800m).
The two gates on this road help to keep it quiet. Round and down the dip over
Crossdale Beck we go up past a few conifer trees, Ringstones Farm, and over
the cattle grid onto open fell (1½km).
We go up to the juction then left and come very shortly to the next left turn
and the layby (600m).
Straight on at this junction the road goes to Bentham (3km).

WALK 9 (Map 6)   *Church, Lowgill, Swans, Higher Lythe or Whitray*
                            9½km or 6 miles.
8 Km roads, 1½km field paths. Dry walking.

FROM the LAYBY

By the left fork over the cattle grid we leave open fell along the walled road to
the second lane on the left signed 'To the Church' (2km).

From CHURCH LANE to SWANS

Along the lane we pass the gates of the Church of the Good Shepherd and by
steep sharp bends down to the Lowgill Road (1km).
We turn left, round over the bridge then up and on to Lowgill (600m).
We go on over Bull Gill to the junction and guide post at Ivah (600m).
We turn right down the road to a sharp bend over the beck and on a few
metres to turn left through a gate onto a gravel road (300m).
The road passes a stone building on the right and on to Swans (400m).
The house is now occupied as a private dwelling and the path keeps outside
the large garden. Through the left hand gate the track goes through the yard
to the right of the large stone building, through a gate into the field, then up
through another gate and alongside the hedge and fence on our right (100m).
The track becomes vague but the route goes on to the corner of the field, dips
across the culvert of Williamson's Gill and up through the little gate just
beyond (200m).
It is easy to be misled here by jumping to conclusions. We ignore the gate
visible in the wall down to the right and bear left over a rise in the field to
another gate in a low stone wall (200m).
There are two routes from here, it is slightly shorter via Higher Lythe.

LAYBY via HIGHER LYTHE

Instead of going through the gate we follow left by the wall side past the old stone building, continuing along a hedge and then through a gate onto a better track towards the large group of buildings which are Higher Lythe (300m). Through the gate we pass the front of the cottages then left and straight up keeping the buildings on the right. Beyond the buildings the track bears right to meet the tarred road (300m).

We turn left along the fenced road past the Lowgill turning and keep straight on through two gates (1½km).

The road drops to cross Crossdale Beck again at Lane Foot Bridge then up past Ringstones, over the cattle grid and joins the Lythe Fell Road (1km). We keep left here and left again to the Layby (300m).

LAYBY via WHITRAY

Through the gate in the low stone wall the bearing is 140°. We go slightly down to cross a ditch then more steeply down but keeping the old building in view on our left, to come through a stile gap in the hedge at the bottom of the slope and on to the footbridge (300m).

Over the bridge we bear left and steeply up past a little thorn bush and at the top of the rise we make for the buildings of Whitray Farm. We come alongside a wall on our right, through the gate and between walls, then straight out between buildings to the road where we turn left (500m).

From the farm gate we go down the hill over Whitray Beck with is grove of conifers up to meet the Lythe Fell Road (1km).

This is open moorland with lark, curlew, lapwing, grouse and sheep. At the signpost we keep along to the left over Green Syke Bridge by the sheepfolds, on over the cattle grid, and straight up to the right of the signpost to the next cattle grid by the stone building (1km).

The road is now between fences, goes down over Balshaw Bridge, then up past Moorcock back onto open fell again at the next grid (1km).

We keep along to the second of two close junctions on the left (1km). Bentham is straight on (3km).

The layby is to the left, and beyond it taking the left fork over the cattle grid, the walled road leads to the Lowgill Road End bus stop (4½km).

WALK 10 (Map 6).   *Layby, Balshaw Bridge, Lythe Lane, Ringstones.*
                                     7km or 4½ miles.
An easy road walk for times when the fields are very wet.
By Car: to the Layby
We go back to the Slaidburn Bentham road and turn right a short way to the next junction (300m).

At this junction with its signpost, the walk goes down the left fork and back up the right fork. Going left it is open fell to the first cattle grid (1km).

Now down between walls past Moorcock, over Balshaw Bridge and up to the next cattle grid (1km).

We turn right at the next signpost before the road crosses the cattle grid and with the wall on our left we cross another cattle grid to a sharp corner (1½km).

This road between the two corners is Lythe Lane and being the highest part of our walk there are good views left over Lythe Fell towards Cross of Greet, right to Ingleborough with its flat top, and ahead over the Bay to the fells of Furness.

Along the fenced road we pass the Lowgill turning and keep straight on through two gates (1½km).

The road drops to cross Crossdale Beck again at Lane Foot Bridge and up past Ringstones over the cattle grid to the fork of roads at the signpost near the start of the walk (1km).

Keeping left and left again we are back at the layby (300m).

WALK 11 (Map 6)   *Lane Foot Bridge, Stair End Bridge, Lowgill,*
Church Lane end. 7½km or 4½ miles.
To the layby 9km or 5½ miles.
Mostly road and good track with 2½km paths which are fairly dry.
By bus: We keep on past the lane 'To the Church' to the next lane on the right (800m).
By car: From the Layby we take the left fork over the cattle grid and go between walls past Aikengill farm to the first lane on the left (1km).

BEETHAMS to STAIR END BRIDGE.

We go along the lane and past Beethams to Foss Bank (500m).

We may be returning through the gate at the corner of the stone building ahead of us. In the yard we bear slightly left and go down with the buildings on our right to a gate at the bottom (50m).

Through the gate we go down with the wall to the stream but instead of crossing the footbridge over Crossdale Beck we keep left along the river bank to the road at Lane Foot Bridge (300m).

Strictly the river bank is not a right of way. The path goes almost straight from farm to road bridge but is eroded, wet and difficult to find. We go right across the bridge then up the road through two gates and turn right opposite the signpost at the first road junction (700m).

Down the road we turn left at the signpost at Ivah farm, along and round the corner past Swans gateway and then down to Stair End Bridge (1½km).

STAIR END BRIDGE to LOWGILL.

Over the bridge the River Hindburn is on our right and we follow it to Millbeck Foot where the road turns left, but we leave the road at the corner and through a gate we follow a track with the river still on our right (300m).

Along the track we cross a stream then through a gate where the track can be seen climbing slightly left through a gap in a broken wall (500m).

Up and slightly left, then down passing to the right of an old barn, we go over a small stream and follow the traces of an old wall towards a gate where the track goes into trees (400m).

Immediately before the gate we turn right, down to the right of an electricity pole, then left below the next pole *photo 26 on page 38* down to a footbridge over the River Hindburn again at a large holly tree (300m).

From here we make across to the gate at the far end of the wall, keeping around to the right or the left to avoid a wet area (200m).

A track goes through the gate and then doubles back through the wood but it is wet underfoot at most times and it is better to use the stile to the left of the gate. Over the stile we climb shortly but steeply through the wood to join the track above and over the stile by the gate into the field beyond (100m).

This is a long narrow strip of field leading up towards the houses of Lowgill. As the field becomes very narrow a short fence crosses and there is a stile on the left in the corner (200m).

Over the stile a fence goes off to our left but we keep straight across the field to the wall corner and follow up with the wall on our right to a gate onto the road near the Methodist Church (200m).

> Unpleasant livestock or hay crop can be avoided by continuing up the narrow field to meet the road near the war memorial, but it is not a right of way (300m).

LOWGILL to LAYBY

This is Lowgill. We turn left along the road which is also the course of the Roman Road, then beyond the school we go round to the right and down to the bridge (800m).

Round the corner we go through a gateway between the cottage and the old building to the right of it, then up by steep cobbled bends to the church gate (200m).

There are two routes from here, the first is more convenient for the bus.

> We continue along the lane to the junction (800m).
> To the left is the bus stop at Lowgill Road End (3km).
> To the right, along and over the cattle grid is the layby (2km).

The second route goes through a stile by the right hand side of the church gate.

> We keep along outside the churchyard wall and the old school building beyond to go through a gate into the field (200m).
> Keeping over to the right we cross a fence by a footbridge and a second fence by a stile, then making over to the left, we head for the left side of a stone building at Foss Bank (500m).
> We go through a gate at the left corner of the stone building and go left along the farm road over the cattle grid to the road junction (500m).
> To the right is the layby (1km).

Photo 27. A footbridge in Whitendale.

MAP 7 SALTER FELL   MAP 8 CROASDALE FELL

This is all open fell country. The northern map is mostly rough grassland whilst on the southern map there is much heather and whinberry and possibly a patch of cloudberry in a favoured spot. This southern area used to be Yorkshire and the old county boundary followed a fence between the heads of Roeburndale and Whitendale. Crossing this high land is the old Hornby Road once an important route with mileposts and wayside crosses. The central portion of the route is easy to follow. Between House of Croasdale and High Salter the track is in parts hard smooth gravel and in other parts it is boggy peat, but the bad portions can be avoided on foot. Although a public road there is no possibility at all of getting a car across the top. A few will venture a little way at either end if they are adventurous or happen to be driving someone else's car, but a wet peat hollow at the north end and the bouldery climb around the quarry at Baxton Fell End leaves the major portion to be enjoyed by the walker, the sheep and a few horses. There is no real summit to the track, in fact it drops slightly across the col at the head of Whitendale and Roeburndale. Here is the old county gate.

From the south the track follows the old Roman Road from the shoulder of Low Fell just south of House of Croasdale, and leaves it just before the old county gate. The Roman Road is about 50m further up the fence at the gate, and bends right to cross two fences before going straight down Botton Head Fell. Just beyond the second fence it is clearly visible as a terraced grass shelf for about 100m but soon becomes vague and does not really show itself with any certainty until it crosses Dale Beck at the bottom. All this is a gentle trespass of course, there is no right of way off the track.

WALK 12   *HORNBY ROAD over SALTER FELL*
(Maps 5, 7, 8, 9, 10, 12)
This is a long walk with a variety of starting and finishing points. At the north end the choice is Brookhouse, Hornby or Wray. At the south end the choice is Dunsop Bridge, Slaidburn or Newton.

GOING SOUTH

HORNBY to HIGH SALTER (Map 5) 6½km or 4 miles
Leaving the main road at the bend we go over the railway bridge to the crossroads where there is ample parking space. Straight on up, the road is signposted 'Roeburndale West' and goes over Whit Moor, steeply down over the River Roeburn and then steeply up by Low Salter and Middle Salter to High Salter.

WRAY to HIGH SALTER (Map 5) 6km or 4 miles
Signposted 'Roeburndale West' the road leaves the village near the post office. It goes up and over Whit Moor, steeply down over the River Roeburn and then steeply up by Low Salter and Middle Salter to High Salter.

BROOKHOUSE to HIGH SALTER 9km or 5½ miles.
The Littledale Road climbs steadily then levels to a bend. Just before the bend we turn sharp left along Roeburndale Road (2km).
We climb again to a double bend near the old brickworks (1½km).
We continue to climb passing the road junction on our right (1½km).
The road then levels out and drops round a bend (1km).
Along beyond the bend but before Winder Farm is a gate on the right (200m). (Map 5).
Through the gate a straight gravel road goes down, bends to cross a beck and goes up to Haylots where it turns left through a gate just before the farm (1km).
We follow the road through the gate and down to the River Roeburn (700m).
We cross the river by a culvert which replaces the old 'Drunken Bridge' just downstream, and follow the road up to meet the Hornby Road at a gate (400m).
We turn right up the road passing Middle Salter to High Salter (1km).

HIGH SALTER to the OLD COUNTY GATE 6km or 4 miles
The track is easy to follow. It goes through Middle Gate (1km).
Now fairly level (Map 7) to another gate (2km).
Now left around the top of Alderstone Bank, a bouldery slope below the track. The obvious track across the valley is a private shooting track. Fairly level again we pass the small lump of Guide Hill to the gate (Map 8) (3km).

OLD COUNTY GATE to HOUSE OF CROASDALE 5km or 3 miles.
We pass Shooters Clough (Map 8) where the beck crosses the road (1km).
We keep fairly level through a gate (1km).

Then steadily downhill to the quarry at Baxton Fell End (1½km).
Steeply down and up to pass a tree on the roadside (1km).
On the left 200m further on is a level path to House of Croasdale (500m) (Map 9) or keep along the track.

HOUSE OF CROASDALE to SLAIDBURN by path via Croasdale House.
4½km or 3 miles.

We follow the directions on page 52.

HOUSE OF CROASDALE to SLAIDBURN by road 6km or 4 miles
We keep on the track leaving the fell at the third gate (1km).
We follow the road down then up around bends to a junction (3km).
Then left to Slaidburn (2km) (Map 9, 12).

HOUSE OF CROASDALE to SLAIDBURN by road and path via Myttons (Map 9, 12) 5km or 3 miles.
Keeping along the track we leave the fell at the third gate (1km).
Then down the road past Woodhouse farm and Lanshaw farm (2km) (Map 12)
The road crosses Dunsop Brook and bends left up to a right hand corner (150m).
We take the right hand one of two gates at the corner and go along the farm road with the wall on our left to Myttons (200m).
We bear right past the first building and through a gateway onto a track, following with the wall on our left into the field where the track fades out and we keep left around the corner of the wall (100m).
The wall is straight to a gate at the end (200m).
Through the gate we go diagonally across the field towards the left hand end of the wall to a stone slab footbridge and steps in the wall (150m).
Left alongside Croasdale Brook, over more steps in a wall we come alongside a straight fence. In bad weather the drier route is up the field towards the farm past a large ash tree to steps up the wall onto the road (200m).
Left down the road is Slaidburn (650m).

> The alternative route is often muddy but firm underneath. We follow the long straight fence to Croasdale Brook and then alongside it to a stile into woodland (300m).
> The path is obvious through the wood where it can be muddy, then it climbs a little to come out onto the road (250m).
> Left down the road is Slaidburn (300m).

HOUSE OF CROASDALE to NEWTON by road 8km or 5 miles
We keep on the track leaving the fell at the third gate (1km) (Map 9).
We follow the road down then up around bends to a junction (3km) (Map 9, 12).
Here we turn right and round the corner to Newton (4km) (Map 14).

OLD COUNTY GATE to WHITENDALE 4km or 2½ milles (Map 8)

We leave the track just beyond Shooters Clough and go steeply down to within sight of the Whitendale River, almost at right angles to the track (200°) (500m).

Below at a sharp bend of the river is a rowan tree *Photo 28*. Keeping well up above the river but parallel to it there is no track but going at first through heather it clears as we cross Brim Clough, recognisable by the dead tree just up the clough (200m).

Then we are on a good track, rising and passing a large cairn which is in bracken on the left. Now above the river on a vague track, there is a dip and a rise before we drop to cross Higher Stony Clough with its few trees (300m). We are now in line with grouse butts across the river. Nearly at river level, but about 50m away from it, we follow a vague track to come close to the river and rise a little to go over a stream with trees and pass under a rowan tree opposite Folds Clough (400m).

Now a good path soon crosses a footbridge across a stream and still a good clear path above trees, but then it becomes vague and we head for the round hump of Middle Knoll with its long wall up to the top, to come opposite Gutter Clough (700m).

As the Whitendale Hanging Stones come into view on the skyline up the clough the path, still vague, goes slightly downhill towards a wooden gate in the wall (400m) (Map 9).

We go on now to a good track on and down by trees above the river. We pass a bridge on our right and go alongside the fence, then below trees through gates between sheds, and through the gate in the wall to the right of the farmhouse (700m).

The frenzied howl of dogs we sometimes meet at Whitendale is a little off putting but they are in kennels away from the path.

WHITENDALE to DUNSOP BRIDGE 5½km or 3½ miles.

We follow the directions on page 60.

GOING NORTH

SLAIDBURN to HOUSE OF CROASDALE by path via Croasdale House. 4½km or 3 miles.

We follow the directions on page 54.

SLAIDBURN to HOUSE OF CROASDALE by road and path via Myttons. 5km or 3 miles.

We follow the directions on page 74 joining the road route beyond Myttons.

SLAIDBURN to HOUSE OF CROASDALE by road. 6km or 4 miles (Map 12, 9)

We go past the 'Hark to Bounty' climbing then dropping to cross a stream and climbing again to a junction before a sharp bend (2km).

Turning right and along, the road eventually passes a farm at a bend to rise steadily to the fell gate (3km).

Photo 28. *The rowan tree at the bend of the
Whitendale River.*

The track is a good one through two more gates. House of Croasdale is just
below the track at the last gate (1km).

NEWTON to HOUSE OF CROASDALE by road 8km or 5 miles (Map 14, 12, 9)

We leave the village towards Dunsop Bridge direction and turn right up past
the Quaker Meeting House. (Map 14). The road bends right (2km).
We dip to cross a small bridge, and passing Laythams soon turn sharply right
(2km) (Map 9).
Just around the corner at an old stone guide post we turn left along Wood
House Lane (Map 12) eventually passing a farm at a bend to rise steadily to the
fell gate (3km) (Map 9).
The track is a good one through two more gates. House of Croasdale is just
below the track at the last gate (1km).

HOUSE OF CROASDALE to the OLD COUNTY GATE. 5km or 3 miles. (Maps 9, 8)

We drop steeply to New Bridge and up steeply around the corner of Baxton
Fell end quarry (1½km) (Map 8)
Now slightly uphill then more steeply to a gate (1½km).
The track levels to cross Shooters Clough with its stream flowing under the
road down into the valley (1km).
The track goes on to the gate (1km).

DUNSOP BRIDGE to WHITENDALE. via the waterworks 5½km or 3½ miles.

We follow the directions on page 62.

WHITENDALE to the OLD COUNTY GATE. 4km or 2½ miles. (Map 9).

The farmhouse is the tall house which looks south down the valley. We go through the gate to the left of the farmhouse along the riverside track and through gates between sheds (100m).

The dogs, often noisy, are in kennels away from the path. We go alongside the wood, then keeping on level ground, along the track with the fence on our left (250m).

Past the bridge on our left the track goes on up alongside the fence to go through a gate in the wall (200m).

We follow the track alongside the wall, then leaving the wall and over a small culvert, the track bears right up the hill (200m).

Over the rise the track becomes less distinct and bears left, but we leave it here and keep on up across the field to a wooden gate, probably still painted red, in the the wall corner (200m).

Had we kept along and down towards river level we would have come through a gate with a culvert on the right. This is the wrong route and is a *cul de sac* to the water works intake only, so we turn back.

Through the red gate (Map 8) the track is vague (330°) but level, then dipping to a rise opposite Gutter Clough (400m).

Now level again and keeping above river level, the route is still vague until it goes above a few trees to cross a clough (350m).

It is a good track across two becks close together, then it crosses a deeper clough by footbridge *Photo 27* and on to pass a rowan tree opposite Folds Clough (350m).

Across a small stream the path becomes vague in parts but goes on, and soon down, to river level and Higher Stony Clough, recognisable by its small group of trees just unpstream (400m).

There is a good stone culvert now just before the stream which has changed its course slightly, and over the other side of the river at this point is a line of six grouse butts. Across the stream the route is vague again. It rises sharply to keep above river level, soon dipping to cross a small stream and up over the rise to a cairn just before Brim Clough (300m). *Photo 29.*

Across the clough and on a little way, we bear up to the right just before a small clough (200m).

There is no path but keeping steeply up away from the river (bearing about 20°) we meet the track just before Shooters Clough (500m).

Then we follow the track left along to the old county gate (1km).

OLD COUNTY GATE to HIGH SALTER. 6km or 4 miles. (Map 7).

Fairly level, we pass the lump of Guide Hill. The obvious track across the valley is a private shooting track. Along the top of Alderstone Bank, a bouldery slope on the left, we go round the corner to another gate (3km).

It is fairly level now to Middle Gate (Map 5) (2kms).

Keeping on to the next farm which is High Salter the track goes to the right of the farm buildings outside the farmyard and becomes a tarred road (1km).

Photo 29. Towards Salter Fell from the cairn at
Brim Clough.

HIGH SALTER to WRAY. 6km or 4 miles. (Map 5)

We follow the road over the grid past the stone barn, on down over the River
Roeburn, then steeply up and across Whit Moor and down the road forking
right to Wray.

HIGH SALTER to HORNBY. 6½km or 4 miles. (Map 5).

We follow the road over the cattle grid past the stone barn, on down over the
River Roeburn, then steeply up and across Whit Moor. Down the road we
keep left at the fork and on down to the cross roads, going straight through to
Hornby village.

HIGH SALTER to BROOKHOUSE 9kms or 5½ miles. (Map 5).

Straight on down the road we go over the grid and past the barn (300m).
Along to just beyond Middle Salter where at a bend a tarred road goes through
a gate on the left (1km).
We go through the gate and down to cross the River Roeburn by a culvert
which replaces the old Drunken Bridge just downstream (400m).
We follow the road up to Haylots where it goes through a gate and sharp right
just before the farm (700m).
Keeping along the road we go on and then down to cross Bladder Stone Beck.
The road is still only a rough track as we climb up to the gate onto
Roeburndale Road (1km).
We turn left along the road, bearing up right and then level, before dropping
steadily to a fork in the road (3km).
We keep right and down around the hairpin bend near the old brickworks
then along the road and down to meet the Littledale Road (1½km).
We turn right and follow the road down into Brookhouse (2km).

Photo 30. Whitendale. The road off to the right leads to Dunsop Bridge.

MAP 9 WHITENDALE

The Whitendale River has its source near the old County gate and flowing by Whitendale Farm it skirts the east side of Middle Knoll in a deep valley to join the River Dunsop below the conifer clad slopes of Beatrix Fell. High on the edge of the valley is Stone Haw Guide. These cairns are known locally as 'stone men'. From the cairn the land climbs more gently up through heather, then around the edge of Dunsop Fell it drops down to the ruins of House of Croasdale and the Roman Road. The present day fell road follows the Roman route for a while around the shoulder of Low Fell, and from here the old route heading south towards the Hodder crosses upland pasture below the steep breast of Burn Fell.

Whitendale is in the heart of Bowland Fell country with good walking over the tops or by clear sparkling water, and just far enough off the beaten track to remain quiet and restful.

The walks in this area are from Slaidburn. There is a large car park at the east end of the village just before the Hodder Bridge. The local bus from Clitheroe terminates at the War Memorial.

WALK 13 (Maps 9 & 12)   *Slaidburn, House of Croasdale, Croasdale House, Slaidburn.*
10km or 6 miles.

6km or road with very little traffic, 3km dry walking through fields, 1km of fell, sometimes a bit wet.
By bus or car: to Slaidburn.

SLAIDBURN to HOUSE OF CROASDALE.

We leave Slaidburn by road past the 'Hark to Bounty' (Map 12) and soon go steeply up through trees, then level and bending to cross a stream. Then we go up again to a road junction almost opposite a house just before a sharp corner (2km). (Map 9).

We turn right at the junction where the old stone guide post gives directions to Slaidburn and Hornby. A little way along the road we pass the base of an old cross (Map 12) near a gateway and bend sharply left. The road passes two farms and then rises steadily to the fell gate (3km) (Map 9).

A good concrete track goes through the gate, follows the wall round to the right and along to another gate where we join the route of the Roman road. The track bends left and on to another gate onto open fell (1km).

The wall on our right goes on a little way and then turns steeply down and we follow it to the ruins of House of Croasdale (150m). We drop onto an old grass track which goes through the gate on our right by the old house.

HOUSE OF CROASDALE to SLAIDBURN

Through the gate by the old house corner we bear left away from the building towards a cairn on a small hill about ½km away, and a little willow tree before it. *Photo 31* Sometimes wet through the rushes, but this is the driest route. We come alongside a ditch on our right and follow it down until it turns left towards Croasdale Brook, then we cross towards the small tree (350m).

Photo 31. House of Croasdale.
Through the gate towards
the cairn on the low hill.

This willow tree has a convenient level trunk which provides, often, the only safe crossing of the rather wet ditch in front of the stone wall. We bear left towards the brook and follow it downstream. There is no path and it can be a bit wet. It is fairly dry close to the brook, but better just a little way up the valley side to keep above the rushy land in the bottom. We come to a stone wall and a gate leading to a wooden bridge just beyond (600m).

Over the bridge we climb up to keep high above the brook (150°) making towards the far left hand end of the trees to within sight of the farm buildings *Photo 32* and then drop down to ford the small tributary brook and up right, to the farm (600m). (Map 12).

We come up to the farm between walls on a short track and keep straight on past a little stone building on our right and on along the farm road (70m). The road goes alongside the wall and through a gate at the corner where it goes left and then right again near the newer farm buildings and on through a gate (500m).

Through the gate we follow the road until it bears left and comes alongside a wall (200m).

There are two ways from here, the road route which avoids hay fields during June and early July, and the footpath route which leaves the road here.

We stay on the farm road which goes on to join another farm road, and then goes left to the main road (400m).

We turn right along the main road which is fairly quiet with little traffic and follow it until it drops down to cross the river and up to the War Memorial in Slaidburn (2½km).

Photo 32. Croasdale House. The farm road to the right leads to Slaidburn.

The footpath route leaves the road at the bend and crosses a stile on the right at the end of the wall.

We keep alongside the river to the bend and cut across the field corner to a gate in the fence (200m).

Crossing the farm road we go through the gate opposite, or the stile to the right of it, and keep alongside Croasdale Brook to the bend where we leave it to cross the field to a stile by a tree between the two gates (350m).

Over the stile we follow the fence and ditch around to the right, then cross the field corner to the far end of the wall where it meets the hedge (300m).

Over the stile at the wall end we go up the field past the thorn trees on the skyline, and on beyond to pass a wet hollow to the wall (300m).

Over a stile in the wall we make for the left hand end of the far wood crossing the fence by a simple stile then over a stile in the wall and straight on to the left hand end of the wood (700m).

Over the steps in the wall corner we go through the end of the wood towards the houses of Slaidburn, going downhill with the hedge on our left, past the corner and towards the bridge to find a stile and guide post on the roadside (250m).

We turn right to Slaidburn (250m).

WALK 14   *Slaidburn, Croasdale House, Brim Clough,*
(Maps 12, 9, 8)   *Whitendale, Dunsop Fell, Burn Side or*
                    Woodhouse, Slaidburn. 20km or 12 miles.

5kms road with very little traffic, 4km of good track, 5km of dry walking through fields, 6km mostly dry fell walking.
By bus or car: to Slaidburn.

SLAIDBURN to HOUSE OF CROASDALE.

We leave Slaidburn by the road which goes down behind the War Memorial and cross the bridge over Croasdale Brook (100m). (Map 12).

Some of the fields on the footpath route are cut for hay in June or early July and are avoided by the road route.

The road bends right, climbs and then bends left again (300m).

On our right we pass a roadside farm 'Woodhouse Gate' (1km).

Up a short rise and down again we pass the waterworks road on the right and just beyond we go left along a farm road (1km).

This road bends left and dips to fork right through a gate (200m).

We come near to Croasdale Brook and on through a gate towards buildings (400m).

The footpath route leaves the road around the corner and halfway up the first hill at a guide post and steps in the wall on the left (150m).

We go up the field inclining away from the road to pass a wall end and follow on with the hedge on our right, through the end of the wood to steps in the wall junction (250m).

Straight on with the wall on our right we pass the corner and bear left towards the far end of the fence (250m).

Over the wall by a stile near the fence junction we keep straight along the highest part of the field with the wood down on our left, cross the fence by a simple stile and keep in the same direction along the highest part of the field to a stone stile in the wall (450m).

Over the stile we go straight on past some old thorn trees, following them down to a stile at the wall end (300m).

Over the stile we follow down with the wall on our left and across the field corner to come alongside the fence and ditch to a stile in the corner where the ditch flows out from the wall (300m).

Over the stile and across the field we keep towards the left of the stone barn to come alongside Croasdale Brook to a gate, or the stile to the left of it (350m).

Crossing the farm road we go through the gate opposite and cross the edge of the field to the far end of trees then alongside the brook to a stile at the wall end (200m).

Over and forward to find the farm road, we follow it through a gate and on towards buildings (200m).

We follow the road, turning left then right through the gate and alongside the wall towards the farmhouse of Croasdale House (500m).

The road takes us straight on, left of the farmhouse and becomes a track going down between walls to the brook (70m).

We ford this shallow brook and follow the remains of an old track which climbs up to high land which overlooks Croasdale Brook down to our left in woodland (150m).

We keep around the edge of this high land, avoiding the temptation to come down to river level until we see the wooden bridge which we cross, and just beyond, go through the gate in the wall (450m) (Map 9).

The next portion of the walk follows Croasdale Brook upstream and at times can be a bit wet. It is reasonable walking along the bank of the brook but drier if we keep part way up the side of the valley to keep above the flat rushy area alongside the brook. We follow upstream until opposite a cairn on a small hill, and passing two very small trees, go around the shoulder of the fell to a broken wall and a small willow tree (600m).

The level trunk of this small tree provides a useful footing across a wet ditch beyond the wall.

Where the near skyline meets the more distant skyline we see the ruins of House of Croasdale. Making towards the right hand side of the ruins (282°) we come alongside a small stream which soon joins a larger one which we cross and follow up towards the ruins. About halfway it bends off to our left and we leave it keeping straight on to the gate at the right hand side of the ruins (350m).

Through the gate a level grass track goes straight on then bends left to join the road near a sign board (350m).

HOUSE OF CROASDALE to DUNSOP HEAD.

We pass a tree and go steeply down to New Bridge and then steeply up around the corner of the quarry on Baxton Fell End (1km) (Map 8).

The road goes slightly uphill then more steeply to a gate (1½km).

Due west of the gate is Brim Clough which leads down to Whitendale River. There is a confusion of streams at the head of the clough which are best avoided so we go on beyond the gate until the road drops slightly (500m). There is a large boulder to the left of the road and here we leave the road at right angles (235°) and passing the boulder come around the north side of the clough which becomes quite deep and well defined as it nears the river towards a small rowan tree. *Photo 28* on page 48. We cross the clough above river level and below a dead tree just up the clough (600m).

Across Brim Clough a good track rises to pass a large cairn on our left behind bracken. The track becomes vague but keeps above river level, then dips and rises before dropping to cross Higher Stony Clough with its few trees (300m). The path is about 50m away from the river, comes closer to it and rises, going over a stream with trees and under a rowan tree opposite Folds Clough (400m).

The path is clear now, over a footbridge and above trees but then becomes vague again and we head for Middle Knoll, with its long wall up to the top, to come opposite Gutter Clough (700m).

The path is still vague and goes slightly down hill towards a red wooden gate in the wall (400m). (Map 9).

The path soon joins a good track and we follow it down past a bridge on our right then below woodland, through gates between sheds, and through the gate in the wall to the right of the farmhouse of Whitendale (700m).

We keep alongside the river and then turn left around the green and go between walls straight on alongside the modern farm buildings onto open fell beyond (200m).

A path goes left over a footbridge, but we go up the main track, bearing right then left to a white gate in the wall (300m).

On up and then right, we come to a corner just before a small vehicle turning area (200m).

The shooting track goes on but we leave it at the corner and go straight on and up past a cairn on a narrow path through heather (about 130°) (600m).

At the brow of the hill is a post in a cairn, then on less steeply over heather and whinberry by a vague path we come to a small wooden gate in the wall, 140m along from the end of the fence (700m).

This is Dunsop Head.

DUNSOP HEAD to SLAIDBURN

There are three ways back to Slaidburn. The first is slightly longer with more road walking.

Through the gate the route is level but vague for a while. We go straight out at right angles to the wall (82°) towards the summit of a slight hill on the horizon, well to the right of the fence posts (400m).

In wet weather it can be rather soft walking and it is easier to keep left around the black peat edge. The track becomes visible as we come in line with the fence which is about 100m away on our left. The track goes on along the same bearing roughly towards the reservoir, and over the brow it is more obvious and becomes a hollow track all the way down (1km). We come alongside the wall (200m).

Then we leave the wall to bear left to the road (200m).

We turn back to the right along the road to the gate (100m).

Following the road down we cross a stream, climb to a bend and then level to a junction (3km). (Map 12).

Turning left we go on then down through trees to Slaidburn (2km).

The second route keeps to the ridge and joins the third route after about 1km.

Through the gate we turn right and parallel to the wall but on the drier land about 30m away from it, and around the curve of the wall me meet a strong stream in the hollow coming from a marsh behind the wall (250m).

The stream flows from the wall and then turns right and we follow it keeping the stream on our right. Then we cross the stream to follow the right bank fairly level along a hollow track around the shoulder of the fell (250m).

The track is less distinct now but bends to cross a culvert in the stream and goes on, keeping close around the top of a steep slope (300m).

The track now becomes an obvious hollow track below the top of the ridge, then out onto the ridge with a view across the saddle to the top of Burn End (400m).

It now goes down left to follow the top edge of the valley slope, then crosses the saddle and down a hollow track with bracken on the right (300m).

The third route starts similarly but keeps in the valley and is a bit more sheltered in windy conditions.

Through the gate we turn right and parallel to the wall but on the drier land about 30m away from it, and around the curve of the wall we meet a strong stream in the hollow coming from a marsh behind the wall (250m).

The stream flows from the wall and then turns right but we follow a line of rushes from this corner along to the top of the valley (100m).

We go down the valley following to the right of a stone banking, and then keeping to the top of the steep slope above the stream we follow a hollow path to come around the top of a small clough (300m).

The vague route is obvious further on as it goes around the shoulder of the fell (400m).

The path dips slightly and then rises to Burn End and bears right down a hollow path to turn into the main hollow path from the ridge route (250m).

Both routes join from here on. Down the hollow track to within sight of the wooden gate in the wall we turn sharp right to go down past pine trees to an iron gate at an angle in the wall beyond the wall junction (300m).

Down the field we keep parallel to the wall along a vague path to the house and barn of Burn Side (500m).

We keep left of the buildings over a stile at the gate and through the next gate to ford a small stream (50m).

Along the track we cross another ford and along to the road (700m).

We turn left along the road and around a sharp corner (300m).

We follow the road along and then come down through trees to Slaidburn (2km) (Map 12).

MAP 10 BRENNAND

The tributary streams collecting the waters from below Wolfhole Crag flow either side of Brennand Round Hill where they join to become Brennand River, and flow on through the rocky gorge of Black Dell.

The high round hill of Middle Knoll separates the Brennand and Whitendale valleys, and the two rivers join at the foot of this hill to become the River Dunsop, flowing on between the coniferous slopes of Beatrix Fell and Staple Oak Fell. Further down river the valley broadens out with scattered mature woodland. Here amongst the trees is Bishops House whose white walls and slate roof help to make the Dunsop perhaps the most picturesque of the upland valleys.

The Clitheroe to Slaidburn bus stops at Dunsop Bridge garage. There is some parking at Dunsop Bridge and much more at several places along the Trough Road.

WALK 15 (Maps 10, 9)   *Dunsop Bridge, Trough Road, Trough Barn, Brennand Farm, Whitendale Farm, Dunsop Bridge.
15kms or 9 miles.*

7kms of road (4kms of it has some traffic) 4kms of good tracks, 4kms of mostly dry fell walking.
By bus: to Dunsop Bridge.
By car: to Dunsop Bridge or several parking places on the Trough road between Dunsop Bridge and Sykes.

DUNSOP BRIDGE to TROUGH HOUSE.

We leave Dunsop Bridge by the main road, steeply up over the bridge and straight on to turn right at the end (300m) (Map 10).

Along the Trough Road we pass school, church and cattle grid (1km).

Keeping on along the road we pass an iron lattice bridge (500m).

Up the road we pass Smelt Mill Cottages and then drop down to the conifers at the foot of the Langden Valley (1km).

We keep along the Trough road past Sykes Farm, the waterworks intake on the right, and the old quarries to Trough Barn, a stone building on the right (1km).

Through the gate by the barn, the track makes for the wall on the right, then bends to follow up the wall on the left to the corner of a conifer plantation (300m).

A good track leads on up past the trees, then alongside a fence and on to the ruins of Trough House farm (600m). (Map 10)

TROUGH HOUSE to BRENNAND

We go straight through the yard and straight out through a gate onto another good track (100m).

Ignoring the gate immediately on the right we go forward around the wall to a gate which leads on between wall and fence to the wall corner (400m).

The route is vague now. It leads towards the prominent steep tongue of bare earth up ahead but soon bears slightly right of the direct route along an old bank to go over a culvert at the head of a small clough before making for the fell gate (500m).

Through the gate the direction is towards the left clough ahead, but the path soon takes an easy bend right, then up and left around the clough tops. At the top of the second clough the path fades (200m).

We continue up the slight valley (28°) to come alongside the fence on our right and forward to the fence junction at the summit of the track (300m).

Crossing the rough stile at the junction of fences the path is waymarked and goes forward along a slight depression, taking the left fork, and as the valley bottom comes into sight, the path keeps left around the top of a steep clough to a cairn (200m).

From the cairn, the path such as it is, is known as Ouster Rake and drops diagonally down the steep slope, very soon becoming vague, towards the near corner of the wall in the field below, just before the sheepfold, and is waymarked (400m).

Through the small gate at the wall corner, the path bends slightly right passing two waymarker posts then alongside the fence to a stile at the corner (200m).

Over the stile we head for the larger group of farm buildings which is Brennand Farm. The path goes down the field, then more steeply down by a shallow clough to a field gate in the wall (300m). *Photo 33*

We go across a small field and through another field gate to go behind the farmhouse, down the yard, and left at the bottom to go down the lane (100m).

A shorter route back turns right at the bottom of the yard alongside a low building to go straight out of the farm down the road, past Lower Brennand and along the waterworks road to Dunsop Bridge (4½km).

Photo 33. Brennand and the route over the fell to Whitendale.

BRENNAND to WHITENDALE.

Down the lane we keep between walls until we cross the Brennand River by a road bridge on the right (200m).

Over the bridge we follow the track left for a few metres, then right and up leaving the river behind. The track takes a few bends to a gate in the fence (200m).

Over the brow we meet another track and go left to a gate in the wall (400m). The track goes on to old mine workings, but we climb a small stile in the fence to the right of the gate and follow up with the wall on our left. Past a corner in the wall, we keep up between the wall and a small stream to a stile in the wall corner leading onto open fell (400m).

About 50m ahead is a low embankment which at one time retained a tarn probably to supply power for the mine workings. Although the tarn is usually only marsh, it holds enough water to feed a wet hollow draining down to the stream we have been following. In wet weather the driest route is left up to the top of the embankment, then turn right along it and round the corner. A marker post on the route is visible on a low hill to the east (91°) (Map 9). We then turn slightly left at the post (68°) down to pass another post and straight on towards the conifers just visible over the rise, to a small gate in the wall just above the corner of the conifer wood (500m).

Through the little gate we head towards the farm buildings and slightly right to go down between banks over the brow ahead down to the gated bridge over the Whitendale River where we turn right (300m).

There are two ways to Dunsop Bridge from here. They join again at the waterworks. The first is a road walk climbing around the fell, the second is by track and path along the valley.

WHITENDALE to DUNSOP BRIDGE by Middle Knoll.

We follow the river downstream before climbing steadily around the shoulder of Middle Knoll, then down to join the Brennand Farm road (1½km).

We turn left down over a cattle grid and along to cross a substantial bridge where the alternative route joins again, then round to the right of the building with a good road back to Dunsop Bridge (3km) (Map 10).

WHITENDALE to DUNSOP BRIDGE along the valley

The first start goes via the farmyard, the second avoids it for when the farm is busy with animals such as at shearing time.

From the bridge we turn right then left to go around the green and between walls straight past the modern farm buildings. We keep between walls until we are well past the buildings then come onto open fell and follow the wall closely round to the right (200m).

Alongside the wall and then bearing left we go through a small wooden gate in the wall ahead, and on along a distinct path (300m).

Avoiding the farm

From the bridge we turn right along the road to the first bridge across the Whitendale River. We leave the road before the bridge and go along the wall side with the river on our right (150m).

We pass the old concrete bridge damaged in the floods, and keep alongside the river to the far end of the wall and a small wooden gate by a tree, then through it and up the slope to the path just above us (300m).
It is a good path from here on. The cairn up on the left is Stone Haw Guide. The path becomes less clear but continues level above a few trees (200m).
The path is still indistinct across Stony Clough and by some broken walling but is obvious again further ahead (250m).
The path keeps level alongside old fence posts above a steep drop, and goes on towards a wall. Approaching the wall we avoid the path which goes downhill to the river, and bear left and slightly uphill to go through a small gate in the wall (400m).
On the right in the valley bottom is the small building we have to reach, but we keep up on the level path and go left around a clough, over two footbridges following the aqueduct, and round to the right (250m). *Photo 34.*
Curving left around the clough top we come to the last birch tree and a zig zag down to the small stone building (100m).
We follow the path going left downstream alongside the river to pass another small building and over a stream (300m).
As we follow the track along the woodside, the road is visible over the other side of the river to the right. At the bridge we go over the Whitendale River and bearing left go immediately over the Brennand River and on towards the waterworks building (300m).
Around the far side of the building and on down the valley we have a good road back to Dunsop Bridge (3km) (Map 10).
For the Trough road we turn right at the war memorial and right again at the end (300m).

Photo 34. Whitendale, below Beatrix Fell.

Photo 35. Bishops House in the Dunsop Valley.

WALK 16 (Maps 9, 10)   *Dunsop Bridge, Dunsop Valley, Whitendale, Brennand, Dunsop Valley, Dunsop Bridge. 11km or 7 miles.*

6km road, no traffic. 3½km good tracks. 1½km of usually dry fell, no paths. By bus or car: to Dunsop Bridge.

DUNSOP BRIDGE to WATERWORKS

We leave Dunsop Bridge by the main road, steeply up over the bridge and turn right at the top by the War Memorial (150m) (Map 10).

We pass a few houses then along by woodland over a cattle grid to pass the keeper's house at Closes Barn, bending right over the cattle grid down to join the River Dunsop (1km).

The River Dunsop has had its share of floods and the severe one of 1967 altered the course of the river quite considerably.

The road follows the river most of the way, passing Bishops House *Photo 35* where the valley begins to narrow between Staple Oak Fell on the left and Beatrix Fell on the right. There has been extensive reafforestation on both sides of the valley here almost to the waterworks (2km).

Passing the tall stone building we go on and left of the large low building to a substantial bridge (100m) (Map 9).

There are two routes to Whitendale. The first is a road walk with some climbing and the other goes along the valley by path and track with a much shorter climb.

WATERWORKS to WHITENDALE by Middle Knoll.

We turn left over the first bridge and follow the road over a cattle grid up to a junction where we turn right (400m).

We go up and back round to the right before climbing left around the shoulder of Middle Knoll to drop down to Whitendale Farm (1½km).

We cross the river, then a stream, and just beyond before the farmhouse there is a gated bridge on the left which crosses the river to go up the fell (20m).

WATERWORKS to WHITENDALE along the valley.

From the main building we cross the first bridge and then the second bridge immediately next to it and turn left upstream along a track on the far side of the river (40m).

We cross a stream, ignore a shooting track into the wood, and go on past a small building (300m).

Along the riverside with birchwood on the right, the track curves left to another small building (300m).

Opposite the building, just before the first tree, a path goes back up to the right then left, right and left again to follow the top of the clough (50m).

This is the only bit of climbing on this side of the river.

We follow around the clough top then sharply left over two footbridges following the aqueduct pipe to go around the far headland to a view of Whitendale (250m).

Through a small wooden gate in the wall, the path soon bears right with fence posts above a steep drop (400m).

The path keeps on but becomes less distinct towards some broken walling and across Stony Clough (300m).

The path is still vague but keeps level above a few trees and then is walled on the right hand side to a small wooden gate in the wall (300m).

There are two routes from here. The first goes via the farmyard, the second avoids it.

> The path is less distinct beyond the gate but goes level to come alongside the wall and on to turn left following the short track to the buildings (300m).
> The track goes straight on keeping left of the buildings and on down to pass Keeper's Cottage and alongside the green. Then right across the stream to a gated bridge over Whitendale River (200m).

To avoid the farm, instead of going through the small wooden gate in the wall, we drop down to river level here and go through the other small gate at the wall corner.

> Keeping alongside the river we pass the flood damaged concrete bridge and onto the road at the next bridge (250m).
> Along the road we cross a stream at the corner of the green and just along on the left is a gated bridge leading up onto the fell (150m).

WHITENDALE to BRENNAND

Crossing the river the route goes straight up the fell following a strip of bright green grass which is quite prominent from a distance. Over the first rise the remains of an old track become visible and the path goes between low banks to a little gate in the wall just up from the wood corner (300m).

Through the gate the path is soon vague. It goes left up the wall for a few metres then makes off towards a marker post on the horizon (248°) and continues in the same direction to another post on the top of the low hill where it bears slightly right (271°) towards a field gate in the wall (500m).

Nearing the wall we pass a small marshy tarn and the driest route is to go along the embankment to the far corner of the tarn to avoid a marshy area (Map 10).

The gate in the wall leads into a rough field but we go over the stile to the left of the gate and follow down with the wall on our right, passing a corner, until we come to a fence alongside a good track and we go over a stile (400m).

The metalled track goes left alongside the fence and soon turns right to go straight down over the brow to a gate (400m).

The track takes a bend or two down to river level and there turns left a few metres to a substantial bridge with gates (200m).

Left over the bridge a lane leads up to Brennand Farm where we keep straight on alongside a long low building on our left and straight out onto the road (200m).

BRENNAND to DUNSOP BRIDGE

The road follows the Brennand River to Lower Brennand farm, climbs a little to the Whitendale junction, then down to the right to the water works (1½km). From here the route is along the road around the far side of the building and straight on down the road back to Dunsop Bridge (3km).

MAP 11 THE FOREST

Dale Head was well above Slaidburn, yet still some way from the source of the Hodder. Here was Stocks in Bolland, a thriving village with school, shop and post office. Market day brought in the local farmers and trade for the smithy and the New Inn.

St. James Church, built in 1852, was destined to have but a short life, for 1925 saw the construction of Stocks Reservoir. A few stones at the north end of the island is all that remains of Stocks, but much of the stone from the Church was used to build a smaller St. James's, safe but lonely now, against its forest background, for the farms are mostly deserted, and the land submerged this time by trees.

There are only small extends of native woodland in the forest, but many different species of mature conifers, as beautiful in winter snows as on the hot resinous days of high summer.

There are some rights of way and a good network of traffic free forest roads which provide good quiet walking, sometimes between the high dense walls of spruce and sometimes out in the open, dropping to cross wide becks in the valley bottom then climbing again to higher land. Although vehicles are not allowed, there is free access to all parts of the forest on foot.

Photo 36. Stocks Reservoir and the Forest.

Photo 37. The Forest in Winter.

Off the forest roads it is very easy to get lost. Visibility is very restricted and conifer trees tend to look very much alike so that when you emerge from the trees it is often difficult to tell where you are on which road. You need to be a good map reader and have a compass to venture too far off the road.

Near the northern limit of the forest is the grit-stone outcrop of Whelp Stone Crag, once another source of millstones. Further south is the newer planting by the little hamlet of Tosside with its church, garage, hotel and refreshments on the Long Preston road.

Access to the forest from Tosside is by Bailey Lane alongside the hotel, and there are other access points where cars can be left without obstruction, along the Clapham road on the west side of the forest, and further south by the picnic site at Cocklet Hill.

WALK 17 (Map 11)   *Stephen Park, Hesbert Hall, Far Barn, Church.*
                          10kms or 6 miles.
1½kms public road with little traffic 8½kms forest roads. This is an easy walk on firm forest roads by way of introduction to the area. Off the roads, the forest rides vary from bare earth to long tussocky grass but are walkable. A quiet peaceful walk and if we are fortunate we may catch a glimpse of the forest deer.
By car: North of the Slaidburn to Long Preston road from the crossroads is Cocklet Hill picnic site with parking space or alternatively 400m west just round a bend is an off road parking area on the south side of the road.

CROCKET HILL to HESBERT HALL

From Cocklet Hill Picnic Site we walk westward along the road, crossing Park Beck at a bend and just beyond on the right is a forest road (400m).

The alternative parking place is just beyond on the left. The forest road is level and more or less straight, it passes two road ends then along to Stephen Park (1km).

The road goes between the buildings, bears slightly left, crosses a beck, then soon bends steadily round to the right and crosses Hesbert Hall Syke (1km).

The road now climbs to a junction where there will probably be a road barrier (600m).

The road left goes to Hesbert Hall but we will go right here, climbing to meet another road junction (800m).

To the right the road goes over a cattle grid to Tosside, the gate ahead leads to Heath Farm, but we turn left along a level road to a junction on the left (700m).

The road straight on goes past a quarried area then on for 3kms up beyond Dob Dale, but we turn left and go down to Hesbert Hall, a group of farm buildings ahead of us (600m).

HESBERT HALL to FAR BARN

We turn right at Hesbert Hall, cross a beck then down and round a bend to the bridge over Bottoms Beck (800m).

Over the bridge at the road junction we turn left and go along to a corner where the road turns right and Far Barn is just off to the left (500m).

FAR BARN to the CHURCH

We could go down past the barn, but for this walk we will keep to the road which soon turns left down to a road junction (700m).

We turn left down to a right hand bend and right again (400m).

The road crosses a beck then on and round to the right to cross a beck and left again on to meet the public road (1½km).

Left along the road we cross a bridge over Bottoms Beck, by now part of the reservoir, and on to the corner and St. James's Church (1km).

Left here brings us back towards Cocklet Hill (600m) or (1km).

Photo 38. The 'Hark to Bounty' at Slaidburn.

MAP 12 SLAIDBURN

Slaidburn is the largest of the Forest villages. Its terraced stone houses, bright with flowers and hanging baskets, front onto narrow streets with cobbled pavements. It is a quiet place. Most of the houses are 16th & 17th century, but the village is much older than that, it was a village before the Normans came in 1066. The 'Hark to Bounty' hotel is quaintly named after a tuneful hound. It has an outside staircase and the old courtroom where the laws of the Forest were enforced. There are a few shops and the Youth Hostel, Brennand's Endowed School of 1717 and the church of St. Andrew. The church is mostly 15th century and has a three decker pulpit. There are 15th and 17th century carved screens, a Norman font and large Georgian box pews.

The village stands at the meeting of the River Hodder and Croasdale Brook. From Stocks Reservoir the Hodder flows past Hammerton Hall, an Elizabethan building with a stone spiral staircase, and on to Dunnow and Newton. To the east, the Long Preston road climbs over quiet moorland in contrast to the pasture and woodland of the Croasdale valley.

The local Bus Service is operated by Leedham's Garage at Dunsop Bridge and provides a regular service between Clitheroe and Slaidburn. At the far end of the village there is a neat car park with seats by the River Hodder.

WALK 18 (Maps 11, 12)   *Slaidburn, Hammerton Hall, Brookhouse, Church,*
Hammerton Hall, Slaidburn. 10km or 6 miles.
4kms of road, a little of it with traffic. 2kms of good tracks. 4kms of fairly dry paths. A stream to cross.
By bus or car: to Slaidburn.

SLAIDBURN to COCKLET HILL

We leave Slaidburn at the War Memorial, going down to cross Croasdale Brook, and just over the bridge, turn right through an iron kissing gate (100m). There is no path but we go along the riverside to the bend, before the ford, then we bear left to a wall corner and keeping right of the wall corner, follow the wall along to the gate in the far wall (350m).

Through the gate we keep straight on with the wall on our left to join a good tarred road, and turn right to a gated bridge (400m).

Over the bridge we turn left alongside the River Hodder, then over a stone bridge across Barn Gill (500m).

This is the stream we cross further on which can be awkward if it is spate. The road goes up to Hammerton Hall, but through the gate at the top of the road we avoid the farmyard by following the track to the right of the stone building, and round to the right up a narrow field to the middle one of three gates (350m).

Through the gate we follow the hedge on our right on a vague grass track on around the corner, and as the track dips towards the stream we bear left through a wooden gate (500m).

Down a rough track we cross the stream using the iron pipe as a handrail, and up the track beyond through the gate in the wall (300m).

On towards the tall tree we go round the wall corner and through the gate in the wall to follow straight on with the hedge on our left (300m).

We go on down towards the farm following the hedge and wall along on a rough grass track and enter the farmyard by a gate in the wall (350m).

Keeping left of all the buildings we follow the farm road alongside a wall, through a gate and steeply up (150m).

On to cross a cattle grid at the wall, we follow the road past Brookhouse Farm on our left, on over a cattle grid at the wood corner and out to the main road over another cattle grid (1km). Left along the road and left again at the corner we pass Cocklet Hill picnic area in the trees (250m).

COCKLET HILL to SLAIDBURN

The road goes on through woodland (Map 11) past St. James's Church at Dale Head keeping straight on at the corner over a cattle grid on to a farm road (1km).

On and then down over a cattle grid is Black House (Map 12) (900m).

The road passes the farmhouse and on around the corner of a stone building where we leave it to the right and go through a recessed gate in the wall, and straight on, up along the woodside to a gate in the wall at the wood corner (200m).

We go in the same direction, keeping along the end of the wood then following with the wall on our right, through a gate at a bend to come onto a grass track between fence and wall (250m).

The track turns left at the wood and along to a gate (400m).

Through the gate we follow the long straight fence and go through a gate in the wall towards a group of thorn trees (200m).

With the wall on the left we go over the rise and straight on down, through a gate in a fence and down again on a grass track to a gate, then through down to the stone building (600m).

Left at the building we go straight by a little building across to a gate in the wall which leads down the road back again (30m).

Over the stone bridge we come alongside the river, right over the gated bridge and along the road to a gate (900m).

We turn left off the farm road and follow the nearside of the wall. On through a gate we pass the wall corner then bear right to the road and left up to Slaidburn (700m).

WALK 19 (Map 12)   *Slaidburn, Stony Bank, Brookhouse,*
                            Hammerton Hall, Slaidburn. 10kms or 6 miles.
6kms road with some traffic. 4kms mostly dry walking on grass.
By bus or car: to Slaidburn.

SLAIDBURN to CROSSROADS.

From the car park we cross New Bridge over the Hodder, and immediately on the left is a gate and stone steps (150m).

> We can continue along the main road. Up around the hairpin and past the first road junction we fork left at the next, just beyond it. Keeping to the main road we climb steadily up then down to turn left at a cross roads with sign post and telephone box (5kms).

The field route over the steps goes alongside the river then bears right away from it to follow a fence through trees to a wall (300m).

Keeping up the nearside of the wall we cross a fence at the top of the rise and on along again with the wall on our left keeping around the edge of the meadow to a good stile in the wall halfway up the field (250m).

Down over the stream by a stone slab and up across the field under the power line we come to a gateway in the wall at a junction (200m).

Through the gate we bear left across to trees and follow with the wall on our left to steps in the wall at a gate (200m).

Across the field and following with the wall on our right we dip by a few trees to a wet hollow and cross a ditch to a gate on the right (200m).

Through this gate it is dry again across a culvert. Along by the side of the wall and stream we join the farm road at a stone building (100m).

Keeping out of the farmyard we go along the road to an old lime quarry on the right (200m).

> We can bear right and follow the road through a gate and along to the main road (450m).
>
> Along to the left we come to the crossroads with signpost and telephone box where we turn left (3kms).

The field route bears left at the quarry and right at the white farmhouse to go through the farmyard of Higher High Field (50m).

We keep left of all the buildings following the wall and through a gate along a sometimes muddy track (150m).

Halfway along the track a long straight fence goes off to the right towards the wood on the hill and we leave the track to follow up the far side of this fence keeping it on our right all the way up to the steps in the wall at the top (400m).

We cross the field and close around the left side of the wood to a wall corner, then level along with the wall on our left to stone steps in the rough corner of the field (350m).

We follow the hedge down, bearing right to Standridge Farm (300m).

The farm road can be seen climbing to the right beyond the farm. We keep right of the large stone building and down the yard with a small building on our right then round to the right following the farm road out to the main road (300m).

Left brings us to the crossroads with signpost and telephone box where we turn left (1½kms).

CROSS ROADS to SLAIDBURN.

From the crossroads we come to a footpath signpost on our left and go over a cattle grid (500m).

Along the tarred road over another cattle grid at the wood corner, we go on towards Brookhouse Farm but keeping to the left fork and over the stream to avoid the farm (700m).

We follow the tarred road over the cattle grid in the wall and on down towards Rain Gill Farm (700m).

Through the gate we follow the road along the wall side, and at the large stone building bear off to the right to leave the farm by a gate in the wall to follow a rough grass track (100m).

The track goes alongside a hedge and through a gate in a short piece of wall, but we keep on up with the hedge on our right, past an improvised water trough to a gate (400m).

Through the gate we pass a large tree at the wall corner and on along the grass track through a gate in the wall down to the stream (400m).

There is no bridge and it is easiest to cross it with the iron pipe as a handrail then along and up to a gate near the top end of the wall (150m).

Up a short hollow track we go on with the fence on our left following around the corner on a vague track and around a walled corner down to a wooden gate in the wall (500m).

We go down a firm track to the stone building (70m).

Left at the building we go straight by a little building across to a gate in the wall which leads down the road (30m).

The road goes down across Barn Gill by a stone bridge and comes alongside the river (700m).

We turn right up over a gated bridge and along the road to a gate (100m).

Leaving the road we go left along the nearside of the long wall, following it along through a gate to a corner (350m).

We bear right across to the river and along to an iron kissing gate onto the road, then left over the bridge to Slaidburn (350m).

WALK 20 (Map 12)   *Slaidburn, Hammerton Hall, Church,*
Stony Bank, Highfield, Slaidburn.
11kms or 7 miles.
Or via Greenwoods
13½kms or 8 miles.
6kms road, some with traffic, 1km track, 4kms fairly dry walking on grass.
Via Greenwoods, 12kms road, ½km track, 1km dry walking on grass.
By bus or car: to Slaidburn

SLAIDBURN to CROSSROADS

We leave Slaidburn at the War Memorial, going down to cross Croasdale Brook, and just over the bridge turn right through an iron kissing gate (100m) (Map 12).

There is no path but we go alongside the river to the bend and then bear left to a wall corner, keeping right of the corner and following the wall along to the gate in the far wall (350m).

Through the gate we keep straight on with the wall on our left to join a good tarred road and turn right to a gated bridge (400m).

Over the bridge we turn left alongside the River Hodder and on over Barn Gill by a stone bridge (500m).

The road goes up to Hammerton Hall, but through the gate at the top of the road we avoid the farmyard by following the track to the right of the stone building and round to the right up a narrow field to the left one of three gates (350m).

Up the grass with the wall on our right we go through a gate in the fence (250m).

On along the wall over the rise towards woodland we go through a gate in the wall and on alongside a straight fence (350m).

Through a gate we follow a grass track between fence and wall by woodland. The track turns sharp right away from the wood and we follow it between fence and wall to a gate at a bend in the wall (500m).

Through into the field we keep straight on with the wall on our left to a small wood, through a gate at the wood corner and down the woodside to the farm (450m).

Through the gate we turn left and follow the road past the farmhouse, over the cattle grid (100m).

On along the road there are good views over Stocks Reservoir (Map 11) to the upper reaches of the Hodder. The road goes over a cattle grid onto the main road and we keep straight on with St. James's Church on our left (800m).

The main road goes through pleasant woodland to a sharp right hand corner (1km). (Map 12).

Here is Cocklet Hill picnic site in the trees to the left, and on along the road is a crossroads with guide post and telephone box (800m).

From here there are three ways back to Slaidburn, the longer road, the shorter road, and the footpath route.

SLAIDBURN via Greenwoods

The longer road is quieter over moorland and goes straight on up the road with several bends to the next guide post (2km).

We turn sharp right towards 'Trough of Bowland and Slaidburn' to another guide post at a cross roads (3km).

Left goes to Slaidburn (2km).

SLAIDBURN via Stony Bank.

The shorter road has some traffic but plenty of wild roses and meadowsweet. We turn right at the telephone box climbing past Lower Stony Bank then down again to a cross roads with guide post (3km).

Straight on we come to Slaidburn (2km).

SLAIDBURN by footpath

The footpath route turns right at the telephone box. We follow the road to the top of the hill just beyond the layby (1½km).

Here we turn right and steeply down to Standridge Farm (300m).

The road bends right along the level then left up the yard with a small building on our left and past the end of the main building out to a field (50m).

With no path we bear right up the field to the right hand end of the wall where it meets the hedge at the field corner, and over stone steps in the wall (300m).

Keeping the wall on our right we follow it to the corner, straight on along the right hand edge of the wood, and straight on across the field to steps in the wall between two small thorn bushes (400m).

We follow the straight fence down to meet a sometimes muddy farm track and turn left to the farmyard of Higher High Field (500m).

We keep right of all the buildings and follow the wall round to the white stone farmhouse and sharp left to a better road (100m).

We turn right here at an old lime quarry and down to Lower High Field leaving the road as it turns into the farmyard, and keeping left of the stone building, we follow the stream and wall down to a wooden gate in the wall (300m).

Through the gate we turn left and follow along the far side of the wall to steps at a gate (200m).

Over the steps we follow the power line down, then left along the nearside of the wall and through a gate in the field corner (200m).

To the left we head for the buildings of Slaidburn visible ahead across the field, then cross a stone slab over a stream and up through a stone stile in the wall (200m).

Following the wall down to the right we keep around the meadow side to go over a fence and down the wall side to the bottom (250m).

On along the hedge and through trees to come alongside the river, the path is more definite and it follows the riverside to a stone stile onto the road (300m).

We turn right over the bridge to Slaidburn (150m).

WALK 21 (Map 12)   *Stony Bank, Greenwoods, Tinklers,*
8km or 5 miles.
For wet weather this walk is all on roads. A moorland walk with some traffic.
To and from Slaidburn an extra 4 kms.
By bus: to Slaidburn
By car: to Slaidburn or the layby near Standridge farm road on a summit of the B6478.

From SLAIDBURN.

We leave by New Bridge over the Hodder and up around the hairpin to the second road junction and bear right at the guide post (2km).

From the LAYBY

We walk west towards Slaidburn to the first road junction, which has a guide post, and turn sharp back to the left (1½km).

This is the Bolton by Bowland road which goes on to Greenwoods where it dips and bends sharp left and right along to a road junction and a guide post (3km).

We turn sharp back to the left on the 'Clapham and Long Preston' road which eventually drops down to a cross roads with guide post and telephone box (2km). (Map 12 again).

Turning left here we climb past Lower Stony Bank to the layby (1½km).

On down the road we go straight on at two road junctions back to Slaidburn. There is some traffic but plenty of wild roses and meadowsweet as compensation in summer (3½km).

WALK 22 (Map 12, 9)   *Slaidburn, Myttons, Ellerbeck, Slaidburn.*
4km or 2½ miles.
A short walk. 2½km road with very little traffic. 1½km paths, through meadow, riverside and woodland.
By bus or car: to Slaidburn.

We leave Slaidburn past the 'Hark to Bounty' and at the last houses of Slaidburn as the road starts to climb steeply through trees there is a footpath guidepost on the right leading down into woodland (300m).
This path is firm underneath but often muddy and can be avoided.

> The path goes down through woodland, and over a stile comes alongside Croasdale Brook which it follows to a fence (300m).
> We turn left up the near side of the fence to steps in a wall at the field corner (250m).

To avoid the woodland path we continue up the hill.

> At the top of the hill on our left is New Laithes, the first farm (350m).
> Opposite the farm buildings on the roadside we go through a small gap in the wall, down steps into the field, and down left past a large ash tree to steps in a wall at the field corner (200m).

Over the steps and alongside Croasdale Brook again we come to more steps in a wall and a stone slab footbridge beyond (150m).
Diagonally across the field we come through a gate at the wall junction (150m).
Along with the wall on our right to the far end, we turn right around the wall corner onto a track (200m).
We go along the track to the buildings of Myttons and left along the farm road to the main road (300m).
Here on the left is the base of an old cross. The road goes on to House of Croasdale, but we turn left to the road junction where there is an old stone guide post (700m) (Map 9).
We turn left again and follow the road back to Slaidburn (1½km) (Map 12).

WALK 23   *Slaidburn, Burn House, Beatrix,*
(Maps 12, 9, 14)   *Dunsop Bridge, Hund Hill, Slaidburn*
                       13kms or 8 miles.
7½kms on roads, only about 2kms with traffic, 5½kms through fields. A varied walk with not much climbing, along the foot of the fells, and back along the lower land with some river and woodland. Usually dry.
By bus or car: to Slaidburn

SLAIDBURN to BURN HOUSE

We leave Slaidburn past the 'Hark to Bounty' (Map 12). The road soon goes steeply up through trees, levels, and bends to cross a stream (Map 14) (1¼km).
Up again past a road junction we go left around the corner to Laythams on the road side (1¼km). (Map 9)

> During June and early July we can avoid a hay field by going along the road beyond Laythams, over the stone bridge at Eller Beck (300m) (Map 14). About 200m beyond the bridge we go through a gate on the right, and follow the wall on our right, to meet the road at a bend where we go on up the road and round the corner through the gate by Burn House (1km).

At other times we can go direct (Map 14). Through the gate opposite Laythams we bear left to pass the short mast with the wind speed indicator and straight on towards the farm in the trees below the fell to drop into a hollow (300m).

Looking across the hollow we see a stone barn with a fence or hedge going left to meet the stone wall ahead of us. The steps in the wall are about 30m left of this junction. Keeping well to the right of the small brick building we cross two culverts and across the rough field to the steps in the wall (300m).

Over the steps we make for the wall in front of the buildings where we meet the road, turning right along it and round the corner through the gate by Burn House (300m).

BURN HOUSE to BEATRIX (Map 14)

We keep along the road past the farm, straight on through the wood and over the cattle grid, then on past more conifers (400m).

Over the grid the road bends over a culverted stream and goes on to 'The Hey' (400m).

We keep right of the buildings and go along the road over the cattle grid and alongside conifers (200m).

Along the road we go slightly left through a gate in a fence and right again through a wall (100m).

We leave the road here and bear right to follow the fence and hedge on our right through a gate at the wall corner (100m).

Through the gate we follow on down the fence side to a junction by a small thorn tree (100m). *Photo 39.*

Crossing the fence and ditch by the thorn tree we go through a small rough gate and continue as before but with the fence now on our left, taking care to avoid young trees (150m).

Steeply down and through a small gate in the fence we go left to cross the stream (30m). *Photo 40.*

Now sharp right up through small trees on a steep bare path (100m).

Photo 39. Crossing to the right at the thorn bush.   *Photo 40. Through the gate and up through trees.*

Leaving the trees the path levels out alongside the narrow stream on the right to go on through a wooden gate at the fence corner (150m).

Following the fence on our right we leave the field again by an iron gate at the far corner (250m).

We bear right to cross a stream then follow it to the left down towards the farm buildings to join a track and through a gate onto the road (200m). The farm on the left is Beatrix but we turn right here.

BEATRIX to DUNSOP BRIDGE

We go along the road over the cattle grid, past a stone building and on down the road to a gate in the wall (200m).

From here we keep straight on down the road, and straight through the buildings at Wood End Farm onto the road (1km).

We can go back along the road to the left but it is more enjoyable by the river side, so we turn right and down to the gates at the bend which lead to Thorneyholme Hotel (200m).

DUNSOP BRIDGE to HUND HILL

The drive to the hotel is a right of way on foot, and there are some fine trees along to the iron bridge over the Hodder (200m).

Just before the bridge we turn left through an iron kissing gate along the near side of the river to the wood (300m).

Over the low iron fence and the stream at the wood corner, and keeping away from the river, we go through the wood into the field beyond and turn right along the wood side to the river again (100m).

We follow the river bank past the aqueduct bridge (400m).

Then on past a brick manhole where we bear away from the river slightly towards a pair of manholes just beyond a shallow stream (300m).

Through the small iron gate we keep parallel to the river to cross a culvert to a gate (200m).

The track leads on past the end of an old wall on our left (200m).

Beyond the wall we can climb immediately left steeply up the far side of the wall to join the road over the rails at the end of a thick portion of hedge (50m).

Preferably we can go on along the track to Hund Hill (200m).

Through the gate we turn immediately left just before the house to another gate onto the main road (30m).

HUND HILL to SLAIDBURN by path.

We could keep along the road all the way back but this route soon leaves it and rejoins the road near to Slaidburn.

Along the road to just beyond the bend and across a small stream we find gates opposite each other (600m).

The right hand gate leads towards the wooded knoll, but we take the other gate and go straight across a field and through a strip of woodland to a gate on the far side of the old roadway (150m).

If we are in the correct place there should be along to our left a flat stone footbridge where the stream crosses. We go through the gate and follow upstream, keeping straight on at the bend alongside woodland to cross the farm road to a stile in the fence (150m).

Keeping in the same direction it is a little wet at times, but drier up towards the little square fence, and then we follow up the old hedge bank on our left to the wall (300m).

The route keeps straight on but the gateway ahead has been blocked up with stone so we have to do a minor detour through the gate to the left and a gap in the hedge to get back on route. We follow alongside the hedge to cross the next wall by a rough stile at a blocked gateway, and forward with the wall on our left along to the stone stile onto the road (300m).

Across the road by the last thorn bush is another stile which may be awkward to cross, but there is a gate over the rise about 20m nearer the farm. Across the field we go over the stream by a stone slab (100m).

Now up a narrow portion of field to the top of the rise where the field widens and just across is a stone stile in the fence corner (150m).

We keep alongside a hedge, then a bank, to the next fence where there is no stile but it is easy enough to get over (50m).

Beyond is an old hollow path which we follow forward then down slightly to cross a wire fence and a small stream (200m).

In the same direction we cross a field to a gate in a fence (100m).

From here a vague track becomes more definite through a gateway and we go along with the wall on our left towards the far end of the field (300m).

The path should go onto the road by a stile at the wall corner but it is in a bad state at present and it is easier to go through the gate ahead and up the wall side to a gate onto the road (60m).

We turn left for Slaidburn along the road (1½km).

Photo 41. The Forest of Bowland from Waddington Fell.

MAP 13 EASINGTON

Within easy reach of Clitheroe, the Newton Fells, though not particularly high, provide a good panorama of the Forest of Bowland. To the west are Fairsnape and Totridge and the deep valley of the Trough of Bowland. Further north is Tarnbrook Fell then Croasdale Fell and beyond it Cross of Greet, birthplace of the Hodder which flows south through Stocks Reservoir and the lovely wooded valley below Whitewell to join the Ribble at Mitton. At the foot of the Newton Fells it flows by the ancient forest villages of Slaidburn and Newton, with lovely walks through riverside pastures below the steeply wooded slopes of Great Dunnow.

WALK 24 (Map 13)   *Slaidburn, Dunnow, Newton Bridge, Easington, Slaidburn. 6½km or 4 miles.*
2½km or road with very little traffic, 1km firm track, 3km mostly dry walking on grass. A delightful varied short walk by fields, woodland and river.
By bus or car: to Slaidburn, or from the bridge at Newton starting with the second half of the walk page 80 'From Newton'

From SLAIDBURN

From the car park we go up into the village and left to the church (500m). Alternatively we can follow the riverside behind the Methodist Church. On an obvious path and past a small iron gate we climb up then through a small wooden gate on our right in the fence and head for the church. We keep left around the far side of the school field to enter the churchyard through a kissing gate in the wall and through to the road (400m).

We go along the road to a corner where the road climbs through trees and leave it through ornamental gates by the lodge on the left (400m).

Alongside the iron fence we go straight on below woodland on a track (600m). As the track bends left towards the bridge over the river, we leave it and keep straight along by trees around the foot of a steep slope and along the woodside to an iron kissing gate (300m).

Along the side of the Hodder we are on a level grass track below Great Dunnow Wood until we come to a small wooden gate at the wall corner (250m).

Through the gate we leave both the river and the wood to follow the wall side straight along to the far end of the field and stone steps in the wall on our right 5m before the gate at the field corner (400m).

Over steps and a stone culvert then left along the wall side, we cross a wooden footbridge at the bend of the river (100m).

Along between wall and river on a firm path, we go up steps to a stile then along the field side above the river to a small wooden door at the bridge onto the road (100m).

We might take the opportunity to look around Newton before we go back along the other side of the river.

From NEWTON

We cross the bridge over the Hodder and go over stone steps at a gate on the left, then following the river, come left of a few trees to a stile in a fence (150m).

We keep along the riverside again until it bends away and then keep straight on over a wooden fence and alongside the wall to an iron footbridge over Easington Brook (350m).

Around the wood side by the wall and keeping left along a hollow track by trees we come to a gate and onto a firm track (200m).

In June and early July, the hayfield ahead can be avoided by turning right along the track to the road then left past Easington Farm (600m).

At other times we cross the track to climb over an iron fence junction immediately opposite, with an old wooden fingerpost under trees. We cross the field following roughly the direction of the short iron fence (83°), heading to the right of the farm buildings towards the right hand end of the trees on the near horizon (350m).

Through the gate in the field corner we come onto the road, and keep along the road past Easington Farm (100m).

We follow the road to the first cattle grid (1km).

There is a footpath guidepost to Slaidburn on the left and the path follows the wall, but to get to it we have to go over the cattle grid and back through a wooden gate in the wall, to follow with the wall on our right over the top of the hill and down to a gate at the far end of the wall (450m).

Through the gate we bear left following the wall past woodland until over the rise we see the buildings of Slaidburn and head for the stone bridge over the Hodder, down to a field gate, onto the road (400m).

Left down the road and around the hairpin we cross the Hodder again into Slaidburn (400m).

WALK 25 (Map 13, 15) *Slaidburn, Newton, Gibbs, Walloper Well,*
Easington Fell, Skelshaw, Newton or
Slaidburn.
13km or 8 miles.
3km road with some traffic. 3km usually dry tracks. 7km paths and fields.
Riverside and fell walking, some climbing on roads. Mostly good walking, but
a short length of wet fell bottom and one poor stile.
By bus or car: to Slaidburn or Newton.

From SLAIDBURN to NEWTON.

We can either walk along the main road B6478 or by Walk 24 page 79 to the bridge over the Hodder at Newton (3km).

From NEWTON

We go down over the Hodder bridge and on our right is a footpath guidepost to 'Farrowfield' and we go through a gate to follow the riverside (250m). (Map 13).

We bear left across to the wall to go over a stile and along with the hedge on our right which avoids a muddy fence corner where the stream joins the river (50m) (Map 15).

Alongside the river again we go over a culvert, over stone steps in the fence and along the riverside to trees (200m).

We leave the river here to cross a small stream by a culvert and bear left to an iron gate in the fence by a leaning thorn tree (100m).

On in the same direction we cross a field and go through an iron gate in a thorn hedge (150m).

In the same direction again, we head for the left end of a stone building ahead which is Fallowfield and drop down to enter the yard through an iron gate by a trough and go left to the road (200m).

GIBBS to WALLOPER WELL

We cross the road, through the gate opposite by a letter box, and along the farm road to Gibbs. We go over the bridge and keep to the left through a rough wooden gate at the corner of the stone building (150m).

The grass track soon starts to climb and we come through a gate into a field (150m).

With the stream on our left we follow the fence, past a stone gate pillar, and straight on along the side of the field to the corner (300m).

Here we go through two gates to join a road (30m).

The road goes on and up alongside the fence, through two gates and a small wood past New Laithe, to the main road at a cattle grid (800m) (Map 13).

The road climbs to the right past a small wood and over a cattle grid (500m).

The road is level around to the left then up to a dip across a stream and up again to bend right over the brow at the top (900m).

Just beyond the bend we go left along an obvious fell track by an electricity pole (50m).

Further on up the main road on the right is a stone trough called Walloper Well, but the track we take is 70m lower down the hill.

Photo 42. The track divides.   Photo 43. Old Ned cairn.

WALLOPER WELL to SKELSHAW

Across a stream the track is dry amongst heather and whinberry and goes past a grouse butt on the right to a fork where the track divides (330m). *Photo 42*

We go left to a cairn called Old Ned (270m). *Photo 43*

We follow the track, keeping down to the left at a vague fork (250m).

The track goes down across Easington Fell towards the shoulder of Sadler Hill. It dips to cross Skelshaw Brook and rises again through bracken to deteriorate at a bare stone patch above rushes (700m).

At the far end of the rushes we turn right downhill parallel to the stream towards the top shoulder of the far fell (80°) (200m).

We come to a path along the top edge of bracken and keep left. The path becomes a hollow fell track bearing left then straight for a while (250m).

The track goes down to the left to the fell bottom and left to the farm (250m). This portion is often muddy and wet. We could have headed straight for the farm from higher up but it is still wet. At Fellside farm we keep along the side of the building, right around the far end, then straight down with the wood on our left to a firm road (40m).

The road crosses two cattle grids to the white farmhouse at Skelshaw (800m).

There are two routes from here; first to Newton, second to Slaidburn.

SKELSHAW to NEWTON

We keep along the road to the left and follow it down to the main road (1½km).

We turn left to pass Easington farm on the right and beyond, opposite an ash tree, the hedge is set back on the right and facing us is a field gate (250m).

 A haytime diversion for June and July keeps to the road and before a bend, turns right down a gated track to a group of chestnut trees (600m).

Through the gate we make for the highest point of the fells (263°) to a fence junction under chestnut trees (350m).

Over the fence and across the track to the centre one of three gates we go along a hollow path between fence and trees keeping right around woodland to an iron footbridge (200m).

Along the wall side and over rough fence rails in the corner, we come alongside the river (100m).

We follow the riverside to stone steps at a gate by Newton Bridge (400m).

SKELSHAW to SLAIDBURN

We go through an iron gate to the left of the farmhouse near a thorn tree. We head for the next farm visible through trees and come alongside the fence by ash trees (100m).

At the corner of the fence we keep straight on above the rough field corner to the fence and cross it near the electricity pole (100m).

This stile is almost non-existent with boards and barbed wire but can be crossed with care. We bear right to ford a stream under alder trees, follow the wall to ford another stream, and through an iron gate in the fence (100m).

We follow the fence to the left and through a gate towards the left end of the buildings, then towards the farmhouse through two gates on a track to Broadhead Farm (400m).

The track comes across a flat concrete bridge over Easington Brook and keeps to the right around the corner of the house up to the main road (300m).

| We could also turn left here for Newton, past the first farm on the right which is Easington (1km).

The Slaidburn route follows the left side of the wall straight ahead but to get to it we go over the cattle grid then left through a wooden gate in the wall to follow with the wall on our right up over the hill to the gate at the far end (450m).

Through the gate we bear left following the wall past woodland until Slaidburn comes into view *Photo 44* and then we make towards the stone bridge over the Hodder to a field gate onto the road (400m).

Left around the hairpin we come over the river to Slaidburn (400m).

Photo 44. Slaidburn from the Long Preston road.

Photo 45. Newton village.

MAP 14 NEWTON

From the Hodder valley the land rises to the fell side farms of Burn House, Oxenhurst and Beatrix, sometimes spoken of by its earlier name of Battrix, which gives its name to the steep fell beyond it. There are still signs of the road the Romans trod south from Croasdale Fell by Gamble Hole to cross the Hodder near the footbridge west of Newton.

This ancient Forest village is smaller and more open than Slaidburn with neat grass verges and some fine spring tulips. An attractive stone village, many of its present houses date from the 16th and 17th century. Here George Fox preached and the Quaker Meeting House was built, and more recently the United Reformed Church.

There is a garage, shop, post office, hotel, village hall and the local bus service which runs between Slaidburn and Clitheroe.

WALK 26   *Slaidburn, Rough Syke, Beatrix, Dunsop Bridge,*
(Maps 9, 13, 14)   *Hund Hill, Newton, Slaidburn, 15kms or 9½ miles.*
8½kms road, 2kms with traffic, 6½kms field paths.
By bus: to Slaidburn. Bus back from Dunsop Bridge perhaps.
By car: to Slaidburn.

SLAIDBURN to ROUGH SYKE.

We leave Slaidburn past the 'Hark to Bounty' (Map 13).
The road soon climbs steeply up through trees, levels, and bends to cross a stream (1¼km).

Up again we pass a road junction and left around a corner (Map 9)(1¼km). We pass Laythams on the roadside, then dip to cross the stone bridge over Eller Beck and on past the access road to the fell side farms (Map 14)(1km). Just beyond the road junction is a stile on the right (50m). We follow the fence to the tree at the end of the wall and straight on across the farm road to a gate at the end of the wall ahead (350m).

Through the gate we make a wide detour around the wet area at the wood to a gate in the wall ahead (100m).

This gate is the one about 30m beyond the end of the wood, and we go through it and straight across the field to a gap in the wall, or a stile if it has been repaired (150m).

Over the wall if we have crossed at the correct place, we should be in a field with a wire fence on our left. We go across this field to a tall tree (250m). There are steps in the wall 20m left of the tall tree. Over and keeping left of the ruins we follow the broken wall beyond, to steps over the next wall (100m). Across the field, the stone barn ahead is Rough Syke Barn (300m).

ROUGH SYKE to BEATRIX

From the stone barn we follow a dry gully down the hill to meet a track and on to the bottom of the hill (200m).

We go over the first stream culvert, through the gate at the corner and over another culvert (50m).

On up towards the stone barn ahead (255°) through an iron gate in a fence and on up to the barn (400m).

Through the yard by two gates and up past the tree, we follow the fence on our left and soon join the track to an iron gate ahead (300m).

Through the gate we go down a good track to Beatrix Farm (200m). In the yard we turn immediately right, and keeping to the right of all the buildings, we go straight out through a gate and on along the road around the corner (50m).

BEATRIX to DUNSOP BRIDGE.

Along the road over the cattle grid and past a stone building we come down to a gate in the wall (200m).

> A haytime diversion in June and early July keeps straight on down the road and straight through the buildings at Wood End Farm onto the road (1km).
> Left is the road walk to Newton, right is the drive to Thorneyholme Hotel for the riverside route (200m).

The field route to Holme Head is not too easy to find. Through the gate in the wall we turn immediately right off the road and follow the wall side a short way (50m).

We turn left before the power line and follow down the field parallel to it to pass two short pieces of wall (400m).(Map 16).

Making towards the farm buildings across the valley, we go more steeply down following a shallow dry gully to steps in the wall at a large silver birch and rowan tree (400m).

Over the steps and immediately left across a fence by a simple stile we go steeply down through trees to the bottom of the hill (100m). The path we need to join is below us on the right, and leads on around the end of the houses. To get there we keep along past a small stone building then back to the right through a gate at the corner of the wall and along the backs of the houses (20m).

This is Holme Head and we follow the road along past Jenny Barn out to Dunsop Bridge where we turn left past the garage (1km).

DUNSOP BRIDGE to NEWTON

At the bend of the road are the white iron gates of Thorneyholme Hotel driveway and there is a right of way on foot and some fine trees along to the iron bridge over the Hodder (200m).

We cross the bridge and turn immediately left along the river bank, keeping outside of the hotel grounds with the high wall on our right, to a small gate at the end of the wall, into a field (200m).

Keeping along the river bank, over the rails at the fence, then by the river again we come to the aqueduct bridge (600m).(Map 14).

This is the easiest crossing place. The alternative is through two small gates in fences to a nerve racking suspension bridge 400m further upstream. Over the aqueduct along the river bank again we pass a brick manhole then bear slightly left away from the river to pass a pair of manholes beyond a shallow stream (300m).

On through the little iron gate and parallel to the river we cross a culvert to a gate and on past the end of an old wall on our left (400m).

Beyond the wall we can climb immediately left following the wall to join the road over rails at the end of a length of thick hedge (50m).

Or we can go on along to Hund Hill (200m).

Through the gate and immediately left just before the house we go through another gate onto the main road (30m).

We continue to Newton along the road, bearing right as we come into the village, beyond the Parkers Arms down to the river (2km).

NEWTON to SLAIDBURN

Just before the bridge on the left is a small wooden door and we go through following the river to a stile and down steps onto a firm path between wall and river to a footbridge at the bend of the river (100m).

Over the bridge and right along the wall side, we cross a stone culvert and go over steps in the wall (100m).

We follow the wall along towards Great Dunnow Wood ahead to a small wooden gate at the wall corner (400m).

A level grass track follows the river to an iron kissing gate (250m). We keep on along the wood side and straight on around the foot of steep land to join the track which comes from the bridge on our right (300m).

We keep straight on along the track with woodland on our left to meet the main road again and on towards the church (1km).

The car park is along to the 'Hark to Bounty' and right (500m).

WALK 27(Maps 13, 14, 15) *Newton, Rough Syke, Beatrix, Dunsop Bridge, Mossthwaite, Newton. 10½kms or 6½ miles. 3½kms road, about 1km with traffic 3½kms firm tracks, 3½kms field paths. Through fields and by the river. Part of the Mossthwaite track is not shown as a right of way on the definitive map but is well used and accepted. By bus or car: to Newton.*

NEWTON to ROUGH SYKE

We leave Newton by the Dunsop Bridge road (Map 14) and beyond the Post Office turn steeply up to the right past the Quaker Meeting House and on to pass a small wood on our right (1km).

Just beyond we turn left over a cattle grid and along the farm track to Gamble Hole farm (350m).

At the farm we go through the gate and forward, keeping to the right of the last stone building facing us, up through a few trees (100m).

Over the rise we keep on along the field (700m).

At the end of the field to the left a small wooden gate opens onto a grass track at a corner. This is Bull Lane, and we go forward through an iron gate, round the corner and left between walls to a gate (300m).

Through the gate the track goes slightly left to go on through the gate in the stone wall (150m).

Now down the steep grass track is Rough Syke Barn (300m).

ROUGH SYKE to BEATRIX

We follow a dry gully down the hill to meet a track and on to the bottom of the hill (200m).

We go over the first culvert, through a gate at the corner, and over another culvert (50m).

We go up towards the stone barn ahead (255°) through an iron gate in a fence and on up to the barn (400m).

Through the yard by two gates, past the tree and following the fence on our left we join the track to an iron gate (300m).

Along the good track to Beatrix Farm, we turn immediately right in the yard keeping right of all the buildings we go straight out through a gate (250m).

BEATRIX to DUNSOP BRIDGE.

We keep along the road over a cattle grid, past a stone building and through a gate in the wall (200m).

We keep on down the road and straight through the buildings at Wood End Farm onto the road. (1km).

To the left is the road back to Newton but we turn right down to the gates of Thorneyholme Hotel drive at the bend of the road as we enter Dunsop Bridge (200m).

DUNSOP BRIDGE to NEWTON

Along the Thorneyholme Hotel drive we cross the bridge over the Hodder (200m).

Keeping outside the hotel grounds we follow the river to the left with the high wall on our right to a small gate at the end of the wall (200m). We make up towards the wall ahead on our right. There are steps in the wall a little way either side of the gate at the bend, and we go over onto the Mossthwaite track (500m). (Map 15).

To the left, the track goes on through a gate with Mossthwaite Farm on our left (500m).

Straight on we keep right beyond Knowlmere Manor (500m).

There is no right of way behind the house but the track keeps on with the river on our left to cross Birkett Brook to Giddy Bridge (500m). From here it is a right of way. Up from the bridge we keep left, past a copse of trees, and through a gate (200m).

From here there are two ways to Newton.

> The first keeps along the track to the road then left (700m). (Map 13).
> Along to meet the Clitheroe road (1½km).
> Then left down to Newton (1km).

The second goes over the river by suspension bridge *Photo 46.*

> Just along the track we take the first gate on the left and go across the field to the bridge (300m).
> The Romans crossed a little further downstream. We go up keeping left around the first wood to a stile at the fence junction on our right (250m). We bear left across the field towards the small waterworks buildings ahead, over two fences by stiles and a stile over the hedge onto the road (350m).
> Newton is to the right (1km).

Photo 46. Suspension bridge over the Hodder near Newton.

WALK 28   *Langden Road End, Dunsop Bridge, Beatrix,*
(Walks 10, 14, 9)   *Laythams, Dunsop Head, Whitendale, Trough*
                     Barn, Langden Road End. 20kms or 12½ miles.
                     or from Slaidburn, another 5kms.

This is a rather long walk. 5km road, about 4km of traffic, 3km track, 12km path, some of it fell walking. A compass is desirable.

By car: to Langden road end which gets the traffic portion over before patience wears out.

By bus: to Dunsop Bridge and commence the walk at page 90, or to Slaidburn and commence the walk at page 92 'Slaidburn to Dunsop Head'.

LANGDEN to DUNSOP BRIDGE (Map 10).

Along the Trough road we follow the Langden Brook downstream, climbing past Smelt Mill Cottages, eventually leaving the open fell road across a cattle grid to pass church and school, then left at the junction, to Dunsop Bridge where we leave the traffic behind (3kms).

Photo 47. The cattle grid at
Beatrix Farm. We
go left through the gate

DUNSOP BRIDGE to BEATRIX

In June and early July, an easier alternative route avoids hayfields.

We keep along the road past the garage and just up the hill to the first farm on the left (250m).

A farm road goes of to the left by modern farm buildings just before the farmhouse and this leads to Beatrix (500m).

The field route goes through a gateway between bridge and post office.

Along the tarred road with the river on our left we pass Jenny Barn to Holme Head (Map 10) (800m).

We turn right around the corner of the cottages, and keeping close along the back of them to the far end, we go alongside the wooden garage and through a wooden gate at the end of the wall. Then sharp left, back behind the garage and a stone building, and up alongside the fence to a simple stile at the top of the hill (150m).

Over the stile we turn immediately right to steps in the wall (10m).

We follow up a very shallow dry gully, and at the top of it bear slightly left up over the brow to pass two short lengths of wall (400m) (Map 14).

Now we follow up with the power line on our left, towards the left hand farm building to the wall at the top of the field, and bear right to join the farm road (400m).

Along the road through the gate we go past a stone building on our right to a cattle grid (150m).

BEATRIX to BURN SIDE via Burn House (Map 14)

Over the cattle grid the road bends right into the farmyard, *Photo 47*, but we leave it at the bend to go up a track on the left through an iron gate in the fence (50m).

We go up the track alongside alder trees then bear right, leaving the track to follow the edge of the clough to an iron gate at the corner of the fence (200m).

Through the gate we go along with the fence on our left, to a wooden gate at the far corner where the fence bends to the right (250m).

From the gate the path is straight on (70°) towards trees in a rough clough between the two conifer plantations beyond. The path becomes clearer and soon follows a small stream on our left, to go under trees and steeply down (250m).

At the bottom we cross left over a stream to a small gate in a wooden fence (30m). *Photo 48.*

Through the gate we tread carefully to avoid young trees, going steeply up to the right with the fence on our right, then level to a small rough gate at a fence junction by a small thorn tree (150m). *Photo 49.*

Through the gate we cross ditch and fence to continue in the same direction as before but on the other side with the fence on our left, then through a gate at the wall corner and on along fence and hedge to join the road (250m).

We follow the road now for a kilometer or so.

It goes through a wall, then slightly left through a fence, past a conifer plantation and over a cattle grid to pass the stone building at "The Hey" (300m).

We keep along the road, bending to cross a culverted stream, then over a cattle grid and alongside conifers again (500m).
Over another cattle grid and through a wood to Burn House, the road passes the farm on our right and through a gate at the wall corner (300m).
Through the gate the road turns right around the wall.
Again there are hayfields ahead and this alternative avoids them.
We go down the road to the next bend (300m).
We leave the road here and turning left follow along the far side of the wall to a gate onto the main road (400m).
Then left along past Laythams and a stone barn to a gated track on the left (800m) (Map 9).
The track leads to Burn Side, (700m).
The road continues to Slaidburn (2km).
At other times we can go straight for Laythams which is the long low light coloured building.
Leaving the road at the corner, we make towards the wall midway between the stone building to our left and the brick one to our right, to cross the wall by stone steps just to the right of a hedge junction which is beyond the wall (300m).
Now straight on towards Laythams, crossing two culverts in the hollow then over the rise and across to the road through a gate opposite the house (600m).
Here we turn left, passing a stone barn, and then left through a gate on a track (300m) (Map 9).
The track leads to Burn Side (700m).
The tarred road goes on round to the right then straight on to Slaidburn (2km).

Photo 48. Through the gate and up to the right.

Photo 49. Crossing right at the thornbush.

BURN SIDE to DUNSOP HEAD (Map 9)

Burn Side is now a private house with barn and the path goes through the gate keeping right of the buildings and over a stile at the second gate (50m). A vague path leads up the field generally parallel to the wall and onto the fell through a gate at a bend in the wall to the left of the wall junction (500m). Forward and then right up a hollow track left of a few pine trees, then sharp left before the gate in the wall ahead (200m).

At this point looking up the ridge there appear to be three hollow tracks. We take the left hand one, keeping up alongside the steep bracken slope on our left, then bearing right to cross the saddle to the top of the valley slopes above Dunsop Brook (300m).

The track then curves up left to the top of the ridge, then slightly below the ridge along a hollow track (600m).

As the track comes close to a bracken filled slope down to our right, we ignore the left fork and keep to the right hand track close to the top of the slope, on across a culvert, then round the shoulder of the fell where it becomes a hollow track again (300m).

This carries a small stream which soon becomes wider so we cross to the right and follow it along making towards the wall ahead. On level ground past the curve of the wall it is drier a little way out from the wall and we go on to a little wooden gate 140m before the end of the wall (300m).

This is Dunsop Head.

SLAIDBURN to DUNSOP HEAD

Past the 'Hark to Bounty' (Map 14) the road soon goes steeply up through trees then levels and bends to cross a stream before going up again to a road junction where we turn right just before a sharp corner (Map 9) (2km).

Eventually past a farm the road climbs steadily to the fell gate (3km) (Map 12, 9).

Through the gate we bear right along the road a little way then back to our left along a rough track (100m).

We come alongside the wall then leave it again keeping up a hollow track (400m).

Along the track we ignore two rather vague right forks and keeping in the hollow track continue up until it levels out onto open fell (1km).

Here we have a wall over on our right, but straight on the route goes over level land towards a small wooden gate in the wall ahead (262°) about 140m from the end of the fence (400m).

This is Dunsop Head. In wet weather the direct route is safe but rather wet so it is often easier to keep right and go around the black peat edge to the gate.

DUNSOP HEAD to BRENNAND (Map 9)

Through a small gate bear right (301°) along a vague path which eventually passes a post in a cairn (700m).

Then more steeply down a narrow heather path to join the track at the grouse butts (600m).

Photo 50. Whitendale Farm. The route to Brennand is steeply up the fell.

Across the valley as we come down the track towards the farm, the route up the far slope can be seen as a brighter green strip of grass going straight up from the bridge, to the left of the wood. *Photo 50.* We follow the track down, then left through a gate and down again to the farm buildings at Whitendale (500m).

Following the track down by the wall with the modern farm buildings on our right, we come alongside a small green with a stream and go straight on by the wall then right across the stream to a gated bridge over the river (200m).

We go over the bridge and straight up the steep grass slope. The slope becomes less steep and the remains of an old track become visible. The path goes between banks to a little gate in the wall, just up from the wood (300m). Through the gate the path soon becomes vague. It follows left along the wall, then (248°) towards a marker post on the horizon and continues in the same direction to another post on a low hill, then bears slightly right (271°) towards a field gate in the wall (500m).

Nearing the wall we pass a marshy tarn on our right. The driest route is along the embankment to avoid a wet hollow below the tarn (Map 10). We go over a stile to the left of the gate and follow the wall down past a corner until we come to a fence alongside a good track and go over the stile (400m).

We turn left along the track then right to go straight down over the brow to a gate (400m).

Through the gate there are a few bends down to river level where we turn left a few metres to cross a substantial bridge (200m).

We turn left and follow the lane up towards Brennand Farm (200m).

BRENNAND to LANGDEN (Map 10)

We turn at the first building on the right to go past the back door of the house and on across a small field by two gates (100m).

Now steeply up a shallow clough and straight to a small stile at the fence corner (300m).

On up alongside the fence, waymarked by posts, and before the wall bear left to a small gate in the wall corner (200m).

We now head for the cairn visible on the horizon to the left. The path is a bit vague but is waymarked by posts and becomes more definite near the cairn (400m).

This steep path is 'Ouster Rake'.

From the cairn the route is waymarked and goes forward above the clough and along the slight valley to a fence junction (200m).

Downhill all the way now. Over the rough stile the path goes forward with the fence on the left. The fence rises sharply from a large post, and here the route leaves the fence and bears right along a wide swathe of short grass which leads obviously down. We keep down the slight valley, left around the top of two cloughs, then round right again and down as the track becomes more obvious, to the field gate in the wall at the bottom (400m).

Through the gate the route is down the valley to cross a culvert at the head of a small clough, then bears right towards the wall corner (500m).

Past the wall corner the track comes between fence and wall and leads down to the ruins of Trough House (400m).

Straight through the yard and out by a gate we are on a good track (100m).

This leads down alongside a conifer plantation to Trough Barn on the main road (900m).

Turning left along the road past Sykes Farm we come to Langden road end (1km).

For SLAIDBURN

We turn back to the start of the walk and continue by Dunsop Bridge, Beatrix, Burnside and as far as Laythams, page 91, then straight on to Slaidburn.

MAP 15 MARL HILL

Browsholme Hall is a three storey building in sandstone. It is the home of the Parker family who were keepers of the Royal Forest. The Hall is open to the public on some days each year as advertised, but is not open regularly throughout the year.

The land above Brownsholme Hall faces south and is dry pasture with scattered woodland on the lower slopes. On the flatter summit at Browsholme heights are coniferous plantations.

The road from near Cow Ark up past Bateson's Farm follows the route of the Roman Road which went from Ribchester north over Croasdale Fell to Tebay and Carlisle. The route went close to Crimpton farmhouse and west to Marl Hill where it is visible in places, then kept east of Birkett Brook where there are some sections still visible where the road cut through rock. On the north side of the Hodder there is evidence of a zig-zag approach and then the road went on past Heaning and Gamble Hole. The modern road keeps further east over Marl Hill and down through fields and woodland to the Hodder valley and the village of Newton.

WALK 29 (Map 15, 16)   *Hall Hill, Whitewell, Burnholme, Low Thorneyholme, Hund Hill, Marl Hill, Crimpton, Hall Hill. 11kms or 7 miles.*
Or from Slaidburn 20kms or 12 miles.
4 (or 10)kms of road with very little traffic. 2kms of firm tracks. 5 (or 8)kms of fairly dry walking on grass.
By car: To the layby at the top of Hall Hill above Whitewell (Map 15).
By bus: To Whitewell, starting the walk below at "Whitewell to Low Thorneyholme".
By car or bus: To Slaidburn or Newton for the longer walk, starting the walk at page 97 "Slaidburn or Newton to Marl Hill".

HALL HILL LAYBY to WHITEWELL
We go steeply down Hall Hill towards Whitewell to the end of the hedge and a gate in the wall on our left, just before a small wood (300m) (Map 16).
We can keep to the road or across fields.

Keeping along the road route, we continue down Hall Hill to come alongside woodland to the bottom of the hill (700m).
Sharp back down to the right around the wood corner we pass the end of the Whitewell Hotel, and on under trees with the river on our left (50m).
The field route goes through the gate past the old lime kiln on our left.
Straight ahead towards the pike of Parlick we come slightly downhill and through an iron kissing gate at the wall corner (300m).
We go along the wall then bear right at the trees to follow down the far side of the old bank (200m).
At the bottom we pass a house, Seed Hill, on our right, to the track junction just below the small waterworks installation (40m).
The track goes right to the road and left up the field but we cross it to bear right through trees and past the end of a wall to a small gate and steps down to the road at the end of a row of fine beech trees (100m).
On the road we go steeply down and sharp back to the right around the wood corner to pass the end of the Whitewell Hotel, and on under the trees with the river on our left (50m).

WHITEWELL to LOW THORNEYHOLME
With the river on our left we follow the road, below the steep woodland for part of the way, to Burholme Bridge (1km).
We leave the road as it turns over the bridge and keep straight on along a farm track over three cattle grids towards the farm (500m).

Photo 51. Burholme Farm.   Photo 52. Low Thorneyholme,

Through the farm yard, *Photo 51,* we turn left at a thorn tree just beyond the farmhouse and over a stream by a footbridge and gate (120m).

Ahead are two hay fields and the track fades out. We head straight for the large stone farmstead to find a gate in the fence (150m).

Through the gate we bear right parallel to the power line to an iron gate in the fence and alongside the river to another gate in the fence (350m).

We follow the river keeping just above the wall and round to the aqueduct bridge (350m).

Passing the end of the bridge we keep alongside the river to cross a small stream and fence by a little wooden gate (70m).

On along the field leaving the river we head for the farm buildings at Low Thorneyholme through a gate at the large tree (300m), *Photo 52.*

Keeping to the left of the buildings we join the road and follow it up to the right through a gate and along with the fence on our left (100m).

LOW THORNEYHOLME to MARL HILL via Mossthwaite

We climb to a bend (700m). (Map 15).

Then on through a gate with Mossthwaite Farm on our left (500m). Straight on we keep right beyond Knowlmere Manor (500m). There is no right of way behind the house, but the track keeps on with the river on our left to cross Birkett Brook at Giddy Bridge (500m).

From here on it is definitely a right of way. Up from the bridge there is a road off to the right but we keep left past a copse of trees and through a gate (200m).

The Slaidburn route leaves here but for Marl Hill we keep along the track to the road where we turn right (700m).

The road goes uphill, steeply at times, to a summit at Marl Hill (2km).

Returning to NEWTON and SLAIDBURN

The route goes over a suspension bridge. *Photo 46 page 88.*
Just along the track we take the first gate on the left, and cross the field to the bridge (300m).
We go up keeping left around the first wood to a stile at the fence junction on our right (250m).
We bear left across the field towards the small waterworks buildings ahead, over two fences by stiles, and a stile over the hedge onto the road (350m).
Newton is to the right (1km).
For those who do not like suspension bridges.
Keep along the track to the road then left (700m) (Map 13).
Along to meet the Clitheroe Road (1½km).
Then left down to Newton (1km).

Starting from SLAIDBURN or NEWTON to MARL HILL

We follow Walk 24 page 79 'From Slaidburn' to Newton Bridge, then Walk 25 page 81 'From Newton' to Farrowfield then turn right along the main road.
The road goes uphill, steeply at times, to a summit at Marl Hill (2km).
It is a quiet road with hardly any traffic and is pleasantly wooded in parts.

MARL HILL to HALL HILL Layby

From Marl Hill the road drops to cross Crimpton Brook and just beyond we turn right through a gate along a farm track (400m).
The track leads to Crimpton and we follow it straight through past the front of the farmhouse which is on our left, and straight on slightly right, through an iron gate and two rustic gates out to fell land (300m).
We follow along with the wall on our left. It becomes a fence and we follow it along then across a strip of woodland (200m).
Beyond we bear slightly left to come alongside the plantation and follow alongside it to a stile in the corner, and straight ahead along a firebreak (270°) through rough grass, heather and whinberry, to leave the plantation through a fence and over a stile in the wall (400m).
We bear left (245°) towards the limestone quarry to meet the road and a stile in the wall at the fence junction by the layby (500m).

For WHITEWELL, NEWTON and SLAIDBURN

We turn right following the start of the walk.

WALK 30 (Map 15, 22, 13) *Newton, Walloper Well, Moorcock, Hare Clough, Browsholme, Marl Hill, Higher Birkett, Gibbs, Waddington Fell. 14km or 9 miles.*
5km or road with some traffic. 3km mostly dry walking on grass. 1km of rough tussocky fell land, mostly downhill.
By car: to Newton or the layby on the summit of Waddington Fell (Map 13).
By bus: to Newton or to Browsholme Hall starting the walk at page 99.

NEWTON to WADDINGTON FELL

We follow Walk 25, page 81, going beyond Walloper Well and over the summit, or keeping to the main road all the way.

From WADDINGTON FELL SUMMIT

We go down the road past the Moorcock to the next road on the right (2½km). This is a tarred farm road with a power line along side it. We pass the farm buildings on our left then slightly left and right past barns and on up a hollow road which levels to give extensive views over Longridge Fell and the Ribble valley (600m).

A farm road goes off to the right but we go straight on with a wall on our left to a modern bungalow where we turn left down between fences and through a gate to Hodgson Moor farm (700m) (Map 22 from here).

We keep right at the farmhouse round the corner of a small conifer plantation on our right and over a small stream towards the other farm buildings. Here we keep left of the buildings and left also of the yard alongside, to follow a track through an iron gate by a concrete wall (100m).

Through the gate we go immediately left through another gate then turn right following the fence and hedge on our right, to cross a small stream, and along with the fence still on our right to a gate (350m).

Through the gate and straight on over the brow we follow the power line across the field and down to Hare Clough to a wire fence where it meets the stream (350m).

Over the fence and then immediately right across the stream, we go steeply up the slope to level land above. Then keeping parallel above the stream we make for the buildings of Hare Clough farm (150m).

We keep right around the end of the farm buildings and through an iron gate. We bear right along a firm road, and with a fence on our right pass more farm buildings, then on and down around bends to cross a stream by a good stone bridge (500m).

Photo 53. The Lodge at Browsholme.

Photo 54. The route to the right end of the wood.   *Photo 55. Past the trees to Browsholme Spire.*

The road goes on by woodland to cross a cattle grid and left through the woodland. It then turns right and past a small woodland cottage along to the tarred road at a guide post (1km).

Left here goes to Bashall Eaves but we keep straight on by woodland to a road junction (500m).

We turn right and round two bends to the stone lodge of Browsholme Hall at a corner (600m). *Photo 53*

From BROWSHOLME HALL

We leave the road at the corner and keep left of the lodge through a gate, along a track, and left through another gate as the track bends to the right (20m). Through the gate we follow a firm track up the field bearing right to come alongside woodland to a cattle grid at the end of the wood (500m).

The road turns right to Crow Wood Farm, but we leave it here to cross the field ahead (Map 15).

In June and early July a minor haytime diversion goes left for 20m from the cattle grid, then right along the outside of the field, and back into the field through a gate at the top then along the near side of the wood (350m).

At other times from the cattle grid we keep straight through a gate in the fence and it is dry walking straight up the field to the right hand end of the wood (300m). *Photo 54.*

At the wood corner we go through a gate and follow the wood side on our left to a stile at a gate in the fence (40m).

Over the stile we bear right up towards the stone building, beyond the trees and fence, which is Browsholme Spire. At the fence we keep along to the right to a gate at the corner of woodland (200m).

Over the gate and round the wood corner, *photo 55*, we go on towards Browsholme Spire. We keep left of a small brick building to come between wall and woodland to a stone stile in the fence at the wood corner (400m).

Keeping close to the wood between wall and fence we come to stone steps in the fence then along outside the wall to cross the farm road at a stone pillar (100m).

We keep straight on in the same direction across the field, and over the brow the route is down towards the bottom of the road visible ahead in the valley. It gets a bit wet lower down and we leave the field 30m before the bottom of the field over a stile onto the road (500m).

The road goes down to cross a stream then up to Marl Hill which is the farm on the left in trees (400m).

Beyond the farm the road goes down, and on the left is a wall junction with two gates (100m).

> There is some rough fell land to follow so we could keep on down the road instead. It is a pleasant road partly in woodland and keeps downhill, steeply at times, to pass the end of a lane on the left, over Foulscales Brook, to a gate way on the right with a letterbox (2km).

The fell route goes through the first gate and with the wall on our right we go through a gate in the fence and on down the wallside to a hurdle in a wet corner (250m).

Across the valley (342°) to our right is a wall corner to the left of woodland and we head for it over rough tussocky grass, dropping to cross Crimpton Brook and up to join a vague grass track to a gate in the wall corner (1km).

Through the gate we start off along the wall on our left across dry pasture. Then as the wall bends away we leave it, heading for Great Dunnow, the wooded hill ahead, to join a good hollow track at the end of the wood (400m).

Amongst the trees the track goes down to ford a stream then right through a gateway at the wall corner up to Higher Birkett (250m).

We can go through the farmyard, or if it is busy with animals we can avoid it by keeping along the right hand side of the stone building through sheep pens and out through a small gate at the far end of the building to bear left to a good road (50m).

The road goes down to pass the cottage, over Birkett Bridge, and through a gate to a road junction (400m).

To the left is Giddy Bridge leading to Low Thorneyholme, but we go round to the right and slightly up to pass a copse of trees and through a gate (200m). The track continues to the road where we turn left over Foulscales Brook to a gateway on the right with a letter box (900m).

For NEWTON
We keep along the road to meet the Clitheroe Road then left to Newton (2km).

For WADDINGTON FELL SUMMIT
We turn in at the gateway with the letterbox, following the directions on page 81 'Gibbs to Walloper Well' and go on beyond the well to the Summit.

For BROWSHOLME
We go on to Waddington Fell Summit then turn to the start of the walk page 98 'From Waddington Fell Summit'.

Photo 56. Dunsop Bridge village.

MAP 16 DUNSOP BRIDGE

The flora of the river valleys is varied and interesting. As well as the commoner favourites, primrose, bluebell, campion and stitchwort, we can find burdock, bell flower, hemp nettle, marjoram, blue sow thistle and the anniseed scented sweet cicely. In the moister places are the mints and meadowsweet, and kingcups amongst the shallows. Here too are the kingfisher, the wagtails and the dipper bobbing on its stone, or skimming low above the water. From high up the valley the River Dunsop flows by fields and woodland and then under the bridge which bears its name to join the Hodder. The bridge in turn gives its name to the village.

Small but lively, Dunsop Bridge has a hotel, village shop, post office and Leedham's Garage, home of the local bus service. Up over the bridge past the village hall and school is the little catholic church. Appropriately enough for its forest setting, it is dedicated to St. Hubert who before he became a Christian was a huntsman. Further on, the Trough road keeps company with the Langden Brook. This is a favoured haunt of curlew and on its shingle banks in the summer the oyster catcher. South by Mellor Knoll and Burholme the Hodder sweeps majestically through its wooded gorge past the tiny hamlet of Whitewell. Here a few cottages, the little church of St. Micheal and the hotel are grouped together in one of the most beautiful settings in Bowland.

WALK 31 (Map 16)   *Dunsop Bridge, Hareden, Dinkling Green, Burholme*
                        Bridge, Dunsop Bridge. 12kms or 7½ miles.
5kms road with some traffic, 2kms track, 5kms fairly dry walking on grass.
Some low fell walking with a short climb, some woodland and river.
By bus: To Dunsop Bridge.
By car: To Dunsop Bridge or several places between the church and
Hareden along the open fell road.

Photo 57. The lattice bridge to Hareden on the Trough road.

DUNSOP BRIDGE to HAREDEN

We leave Dunsop Bridge towards the Trough, going over the bridge and steeply up then along the main road to the junction (300m).

We turn right past school and church then over the cattle grid onto open fell road above Langden Brook to the iron lattice bridge on the left (2kms). *Photo 57.*

HAREDEN to BURHOLME BRIDGE

Over the bridge we go straight on to Hareden Farm (300m).

At the farm the road crosses Hareden Brook by a stone bridge to the right and goes past farm buildings, and old kennels, before crossing the brook again by a flat concrete bridge on the left (100m).

Across the bridge we go through the field gate immediately on the left and steeply up the field, making over towards the stone wall on the left. There is no path (400m).

We follow up the wall, crossing to the far side of it by a field gate, and continue up with the wall on our right until the track becomes visible (300m).

The track emerges onto rougher fell land through a field gate at the junction of walls. Through the gate it continues to rise slightly to cross a small ditch which is running back down to a row of trees on the right (100m).

The track becomes vague again but level. It heads for the right hand side of woodland visible ahead (222°) and then slightly right through a field gate in the wall (400m).

With the fence on our left we continue towards a pine tree, and enter woodland through a field gate by a larch tree at the angle of the wall (300m).

A rather steep track goes down and then bears right to go steeply up again through the wood (300m).

It can be a bit wet at times in the dip for a short distance. There are a number of signs directing walkers along this part of the route. There is no right of way past New Hey Farm. The track becomes more definite again as it rises above the wood with fell land over on the right (200m).

Much of this woodland is beech which thrives on the limestone. Over the hurdle gate we follow a path through a coniferous plantation which is fairly level to a gate (500m).

This plantation provides some useful shelter on a windy day, with as yet, a view of the Hodder over trees. Through the gate a vague path leads down to the tarred road (200m).

We turn left along the road to a junction (300m).

Almost 2km shorter is the tarred road to the left which leads past Tunstall Ing to the main road (1km) then left to Burholme Bridge (1½km).

We turn down right at the junction through the farmyard of Higher Fence Wood, following the track down to cross a stream just beyond the farm buildings (200m).

Over the stream we turn off left down a narrow field between stream and hedge (100m).

The hedge on the right becomes a fence, and a stile leads across the corner of the field to another similar stile in the fence (50m). *Photo 58*.

We go on to Dinkling Green Farm, making for a gate to the left of the farmhouse (200m).

We go through the gate into the farmyard and turn left at the far end of the first building, *photo 59*, round onto the farm road. It goes over the stream and climbs up then level along the side of Long Knotts to the main road at a telephone box (1km).

It is a little shorter to Burholme Bridge by road.

Turning left we climb to the road junction where our shorter walk rejoins (800m).

Then down to the road junction with the seat at Burholme Bridge (1½km).

Photo 58. Over stiles from Higher Fence Wood to Dinkling Green.

Photo 59. Dinkling Green. Left at the end of the buildings.

For the footpath route from Dinkling Green road end, we come through the gate and straight along the road opposite, and just past the farm track is a footbridge and stile on the left (250m) (Map 21).

Over the fence we make for the middle one of three grey buildings, to go around the right hand end of the nearest one and left through a gate (300m). Passing between the corner of the stone building and the large modern one, we bear right through a gate to the farm road and left to Fair Oak farmhouse (70m).

Just beyond the farmhouse we bear right down a track and over a culvert to a gate (100m).

We follow the track by the wall until it fades out beyond the wall corner then head towards the wooded knoll of Kitcham Hill on the skyline, to a gate in the fence (300m).

Through the gate we follow the wall along the side of the meadow and 20m along to the right of the corner we climb a wooden stile in the wall (150m).

We climb the shoulder of the fell keeping over to the right (60°) through scattered limestone outcrop (150m).

Over the brow we head for Burholme Bridge in the middle distance, keeping just left of the trees in the valley bottom to come onto a track alongside a stream (450m).

We follow through gates into the farmyard, *photo 60,* and by two tall cylindrical metal hoppers then left along the tarred road out of the farm (100m).

We follow the road along and through trees to a grass triangle with a milk stand (600m) (Map 16).

Here we turn right by woodland along to the road junction with the seat at Burholme Bridge (600m). There are two ways to Dunsop Bridge.

Photo 60. New Laund. Past the hoppers and left along the road.

Photo 61. Langden Bridge and the Hodder.

BURHOLME BRIDGE to DUNSOP BRIDGE by road

The road to the left goes over Langden Bridge to a road junction and signpost, *photo 62,* (2km).
Hareden is on and round to the left (2km).
Dunsop Bridge is along the straight road to the right (300m).

BURHOLME BRIDGE to DUNSOP BRIDGE by path

We go over the bridge and turn left over a cattle grid along a farm road with the river on the left, and over two more cattle grids, on towards the farm (500m).
We follow the road through the farm yard, and round to the left beyond the farmhouse by a neatly walled thorn tree then over the stream by a footbridge and a gate (120m).
Just through the gate the track fades out in meadow land. Ahead is a large stone farmstead and we head straight for it to find a gate in a fence (150m).
Through the gate we bear right, parallel to the power line to an iron gate in a fence and alongside the river to another gate in a fence (350m).
Alongside the river again we keep just above the stone wall. Here to our left the Langden Brook flows under Langden Bridge to join the Hodder. *Photo 61.* We go on under the power line to the aqueduct bridge (350m).
There are two routes from here.
The first crosses the river and goes via Root Farm.

Across the aqueduct bridge we keep alongside the river to the start of the wall. Here we leave the river and follow the wall to the left under the power line and through the gate in the fence, to follow the wall side on a firm track (300m).
The track bends left and right to follow the wall then through a gate in a fence to ornamental iron gates in the wall leading into the farmyard (250m).

Photo 62. Signpost dated 1739. Dunsop Bridge.   *Photo 63. Behind the building, along the river bank.*

We turn left to go around the corner of the modern building and then follow the road alongside the main buildings out over the cattle grid to the main road (200m).
Down over the bridge is Dunsop Bridge.
Up to the left and straight along the main road to the signpost then right past school and church leads back to Hareden (2km).

The second route keeps to the nearside of the river via Thorneyholme.
Past the bridge we keep alongside the river to cross a stream and fence at a little wooden gate (70m).
On alongside the river we go through an old iron kissing gate and cross a stream (100m).
Following the riverside we eventually join the farm road alongside the wall but leave it to go along the river bank, behind the small building, *photo 63,* and over the bridge (500m).
Along the drive we meet the road and turn left to Dunsop Bridge (300m).
The road goes along by the river, over the bridge, steeply up and straight along to the signpost, then right past school and church to Hareden (2km).

WALK 32 (Map 14, 16) *Dunsop   Bridge,   Root,   Low   Thorneyholme, Aqueduct, Thorneyholme, Dunsop Bridge. 3km or 2 miles.*
No road. 1½km of tracks. 1½km on grass. A short walk mostly by the riverside.
By bus or car: to Dunsop Bridge.

We go up over the bridge towards the Trough but half way up the hill at the bend we turn in at the farm road under trees on the left, and over the cattle grid to Root Farm (Map 16) (150m).

The road leads alongside the older stone buildings to a large modern building at the end and we go round the corner of this building and out through ornamental iron gates in the wall (100m).

The firm track continues along with the wall on our left, through a gate in a fence and on with the wall bending left then right to the far corner where the fence commences (250m).

The track fades out but we go through a gate in the fence following the wall then turning right alongside the river to the aqueduct bridge ahead (300m). Across the Hodder over the bridge we turn left to cross a small stream and fence at a little wooden gate (70m).

Along the field leaving the river side, we head for the buildings of Low Thorneyholme, through a gate at the large tree (300m). *Photo 52. (Page 96).* Keeping to the left of the buildings we join the road and follow it up to the right through a gate and along with the fence on our left (100m).

We climb to a bend and on our left is a gate in a wall with a stile just before it (Map 14) (700m).

Over the stile we go down to cross the River Hodder by the aqueduct bridge and turn left to follow the far side of the river (200m).

We follow with the river on our left around the bend to the small wood (400m).

Keeping along the fence side we find an easy way through it into the wood then go across the wood to the river again (100m).

Close to the river we cross the stream and the low iron fence and keep along the river bank again to an iron kissing gate onto the Thorneyholme drive and turn right to the main road and Dunsop Bridge (450m).

WALK 33 (Map 16, 20, 21) *Chipping, Lickhurst, Dinkling Green, Hareden, Dunsop Bridge, Burholme Bridge, Greystonely, Loud Mythom, Chipping. 19km or 12 miles.*
6½km road, some with traffic. 5½km tracks. 7km paths usually dry. Some woodland, low fells, riverside and pasture.
By bus or car: to Chipping or to Dunsop Bridge starting half way round the walk at page 110 "Dunsop Bridge to the Aqueduct".

CHIPPING to DINKLING GREEN

We leave Chipping by the road which follows around the churchyard wall north by Church Rake towards the fells (Map 20) (300m).

A road bears left but we dip to the right following the road over the bridge past the chair works to the mill pond above (200m).

The road is level by Chipping Brook and then beyond the factory climbs steeply before levelling again to a junction (1km).

A road goes steeply down on the left but we keep straight on up past Bradley Barn and level again by Saddle gate (1km).

Photo 64. Between buildings at Dinkling Green Farm.   *Photo 65. Out by the gate at Dinkling Green Farm.*

We come alongside a stream on our left and on to a gate onto open fell, then along the tarred road to a junction (500m). We turn right here on a rough track past Jenny Hey Barn to a ford (600m).

The track is over a low hill called Stanley to a right hand bend (650m) (Map 21).

From here it follows parallel to Rathera Clough towards Lickhurst farm (750m).

Keeping left of the farm buildings at Lickhurst we go down the road to cross a ford at the bottom, then follow the road round to the right and along by a stream to cross a second ford, through an iron gate and across a third ford in quick succession (450m).

From the ford we go up and along just past the phone box to the road junction (300m).

On the left is a gate and we follow a firm track through the gate, on over cattle grids, then down to Dinkling Green Farm (Map 16) (1km).

DINKLING GREEN to DUNSOP BRIDGE

At the farm, *photo 64,* the track leads between two buildings, the one on our right having a small brick addition, and in the yard we turn immediately right to a field gate at the end of the buildings (60m). *Photo 65.*

We cross the field due north to a simple stile in the fence (200m).

Across the corner of the field we find a similar stile in the fence (50m).

Over the stile we go left along the narrow field with the hedge on our left to meet a good track (200m).

Turning right along the track we cross a stream, on through the farmyard of Higher Fence Wood and up the short tarred road to turn left at the road junction (250m).

We go along the road to a dip over the stream where the road turns left (300m).

Leaving the road at the bend we climb to the right along a vague path to enter a conifer plantation at a field gate (200.⸱.).

Through the gate we keep along the left fork and again further on we keep along the left fork maintaining a fairly level walk on grass to a wooden hurdle gate at the end of the plantation (500m).

Over the gate we follow a track above beech trees with the fell over the fence on our left, then the track goes down more steeply through trees (300m).

This portion of the track can be rather wet at times in the dip but becomes dry and climbs to the left fairly steeply on an old track to a gate at the wall corner by a larch tree (200m).

This portion of the walk is under trees all the way and does not come into the open fields below. There is no right of way down past New Hey Farm.

Through the gate we follow with the wall on our right past a pine tree by a small stream then further on by a vague track bearing slightly left to a field gate in the wall ahead (300m).

Through the gate we make for the left side of Mellor Knoll which is the round hill ahead on the right (42°). This is level walking on grass but no track until we get near to Mellor Knoll where the track leads around the end of a row of trees below, to a gate at a wall junction (500m).

We follow the track down with a wall on our left. It fades out but we keep along the wall side and through a gate to continue along the far side of the same wall (600m).

As the slope gets steeper we come in sight of 'Hareden Cottage' a detached stone house in the valley bottom. *Photo 66.*

We make for the field gate to the right of the cottage and over a flat concrete bridge across Hareden Brook (200m).

We follow the road along to the right past the buildings of Hareden Farm crossing the stream again by a stone bridge on the right (100m).

Across the bridge we keep left alongside the stream following the road to cross the iron bridge over Langden Brook onto the Trough road (300m).

Photo 66. Hareden Cottage and Hareden Farm.

Along to the right the road goes over a cattle grid then past church and school to a road jucntion (2km).

| The road straight on alongside woodland leads over Langden Bridge to Burholme Bridge to rejoin the walk.

We turn left at the junction along the straight road to Dunsop Bridge. As we drop down to the bridge a farm road on the right leads under trees via Root Farm, or we can go down over the bridge for the Thorneyholme route (300m).

DUNSOP BRIDGE to the AQUEDUCT via Root Farm

Halfway up the hill above the bridge we turn into a farm road under trees and over a cattle grid to Root Farm (70m).

The road leads alongside the older stone buildings to a large modern building at the end, and we go around the corner of this building then out through ornamental iron gates in the wall (100m).

The firm track continues along with the wall on our left through a gate in the fence and on with the wall, bending left then right, to the far corner where the fence commences (250m).

The track fades out here and we go through a gate in the fence, following the wall then to the right alongside the river to the large aqueduct bridge ahead (300m).

Over the bridge we turn right for Burholme.

DUNSOP BRIDGE to the AQUEDUCT via Thorneyholme

From the bridge we go past the post office and garage and turn in at white iron gates on the right at a bend (100m). The drive leads principally to Thorneyholme Hotel.

We go along through trees, some are tall wellingtonias, and across the bridge but before we come to the hotel gate we turn right through a little iron gate at the end of the bridge which takes us onto the river bank (150m).

Photo 67. Through the gates to Burholme Farm.

Photo 68. Cattle grazing by the Hodder at Burholme.

We follow the river bank along until we meet the long hedge on our left (500m).
Across a small stream and through an iron kissing gate we turn right to follow the river again and through a small wooden gate at the next fence to pass the end of the aqueduct bridge (170m).

AQUEDUCT to LOUD MYTHOM
From the aqueduct bridge we follow the riverside fence, crossing under the power line, then following along just above the stone wall. Here the Langden Brook flowing under Langden Bridge joins the Hodder. We keep along with the wall on our right to a gate in a fence (350m).
Through the gate we follow the river again, photo 67, through an iron gate in a fence then straight on to a wooden gate in a fence (350m).
Through the gate we make straight ahead towards the chimney of the farmhouse just visible over the rise and come onto a track as it goes through a gate (150m).
We cross the stream by a footbridge, along, then right by a walled thorn tree following the farm road past the front of the farmhouse which is Burholme and on over two cattle grids alongside the river to Burholme Bridge (600m).
We cross the bridge and bear left along the road signposted 'Chipping 5' to come alongside woodland on our left (400m). The road keeps along the wood side passing two road ends to farms (700m).
Steeply up we pass a limestone knoll and on along the road, drop to a road junction near a telephone box where we turn left (1½km).
Just along this road on our right we follow a farm track to Higher Greystoneley (Map 21) (200m).

Keeping left of the farmhouse through a gate we cross the field (450m).

It is a firm track now for nearly 2kms. Through an iron gate into woodland the lane goes down to a shallow ford, or the footbridge to the right, and up again through woodland to the barn at Lower Greystoneley (300m).

We keep along by the small building bearing slightly left through a gate in the wall and on between hedges to a wooden gate (350m).

Straight on alongside on old thorn hedge we pass Knot Barn and along by another thorn hedge to a corner (350m).

The track goes across open field to a wooden gate at the corner of the field and along to the road (600m).

Exactly opposite is a simple stile in the hedge and we follow straight on with the hedge on our right to a stile at wooden rails, onto the road (500m).

The road goes on then down to Loud Mythom farm (800m).

LOUD MYTHOM to CHIPPING

There are two routes back to Chipping, either side of the River Loud. The first is along the near side and goes over stepping stones which are easy enough unless the river is high.

We go through a wooden gate opposite the farm, 35m before the bridge, and keep along the riverside under a few trees along to a stile at a fence (250m).

On along the riverside we pass a small wier, by an electricity pole, and along to another stile in a fence (300m).

Still along the riverside we pass the remains of an old thorn hedge to a stile in a fence at three tall trees and left over the stepping stones (200m).

We keep right of the fence corner following it up to a footbridge then right to follow the riverside again to a stile in a fence (250m).

Over the stile we go on to Gibbon Bridge and carefully up wooden steps to the road at the end of the parapet (250m).

From Gibbon Bridge we keep to the road turning right across the bridge and on to Chipping (2kms).

The alternative route goes on over Loud Mythom Bridge and along to the right.

At the bottom of the hill we go right over a stile at the far end of a parapet wall (70m).

We follow close to the river and going through scrub and trees we cross a fence at a stile below a wood (330m).

On passing the end of a hedge we follow the River Loud to the ruins of an old barn (300m).

Over fence rails to the right of the barn we cross a footbridge then forward again following the riverside to a stile in a fence (250m).

From the stile we follow the river to Gibbon Bridge and carefully up wooden steps to the road at the end of the parapet (250m).

From Gibbon Bridge we keep to the road, turning right across the bridge and on to Chipping (2kms).

For DUNSOP BRIDGE

Continue with the start of the walk page 107 'Chipping to Dinkling Green'.

Photo 69. Langden road end.

MAP 17 LANGDEN CASTLE

Just below Sykes the Langden valley meets the Trough road, and with space to park a few cars is a popular picnic corner by the river. Along by the road the Langden is certainly a river, but only a few miles upstream it is just a trickle where under Hawthornthwaite Fell Top it has its source at Langden Head, and gathering other streams along the way, flows by Dead Man's Stake and Stransdale Nab to Fiendsdale. It is tempting to speculate about the dead man but it is more than likely that this rather insignificant stone is a natural occurence and was probably named by the man who named Langden Castle.

To a traveller this high fell land is featureless, and in winter snow particularly, it feels quite remote even today. Downstream at the foot of Bleadale is Langden Castle, certainly not a castle, and close by is Holdron Castle, a natural rock pinnacle. From the Trough road a drive through trees leads to the water works, but this is only the start of an old established route which follows the north side of the river then climbs up over Fiendsdale Head to Bleasdale and on to meet the old Roman Road through Oakenclough. Walking in the upper Hareden valley has not been encouraged, but the Bleadale route which for some reason has been missed on the definitive footpath map, is an accepted path which has been used for well over 40 years and provides an alternative route to the access area.

WALK 34 (Maps 10, 17)   *Langden Road End to Langden Castle and back. 6km or 4 miles, altogether. From Dunsop Bridge 12km or 7½ miles.*
1km of road without traffic and 5km of firm track. Good dry walking all the way. From Dunsop Bridge another 3km each way on the road.
This walk can be continued from Langden Castle either up Bleadale or Fiendsdale to the Access Area. There are fords beyond Langden Castle.

From DUNSOP BRIDGE

We go over the bridge and straight along to the road junction (Map 10) (300m).
Turning right along the Trough road past school and church and over the cattle grid we come onto unfenced road above Langden Brook. The first bridge is an iron lattice road bridge on the left, but we go on up the road past Smelt Mill Cottages and on to the conifer plantation at the foot of the Langden valley, *photo 69* (3km).

From LANGDEN ROAD END

Through the water works entrance gate we go along the driveway under trees to the waterworks house (Map 17) (400m).
Keeping right around the garden railings we go up the track alongside the railings to a good stile by a gate (200m).
A great many stiles are awkward to use, but this one is a good design which enables the walker to turn round at the top without getting wedged in with a rucksack.
The track follows the valley bottom to a rowan tree at Mere Clough (700m). Here a short sharp rise carries the track above the valley floor before it levels and continues forward to a fork (100m).
The right fork is a shooting track and goes higher up the fell to join the right of way again at Holdron Castle. We take the lower route following above the river and then bending right towards the natural rock pinnacles of Holdron Castle on the fell side above us (1km).
The track now goes down to Langden Castle, a stone building of doubtful age, but certainly not a castle, which provides some useful shelter in bad weather (500m).
The track ceases to be a right of way just beyond Langden Castle.
The continuation via Fiendsdale to Chipping is described on page 134; via Bleadale and Saddle Fell on page 118, continuing to Chipping on page 139.

Photo 70. River Brock at Snape Rake.

MAP 18 BLEASDALE

Thea Bleasdale Estate is sheltered from the north and east by the surrounding fells. A large tract of the estate lies between the fells and the main road to the south, and this area is open to estate traffic only, but some of the paths and most of the roads are rights of way on foot. The hamlet of Bleasdale is usually thought of as the church, the few buildings around the school and probably the Bleasdale Post Office cafe although this is actually in the neighbouring parish of Goosnargh. The estate is centered around Bleasdale Tower. It is an attractive Victorian building but it cannot be seen from any of the roads.

Some of the earliest occupants of this area were the people of the early bronze age. About 1800 BC they built Bleasdale Circle. There was a large circle about 46m or 150ft diameter and inside it a much smaller one marked out by wooden posts. There is little to be seen on the ground and there is no public path to the circle, but the remnants of the wooden posts and two urns excavated from the site are in the Harris Museum at Preston.

The River Brock has been a firm favourite with generations of walkers. It has two sources both of them in Bleasdale. One rises on the southern slopes of Fairsnape and flows past Bleasdale Post Office. The other, also known as River Brock, flows by Holme House and under Jack Anderton's Bridge. Only a few hundered metres at Fiendsdale Head separates the Brock from its northerly neighbour the Calder which flows west through Oakenclough and gives its name to the deep wooded valley and its village of Calder Vale.

The Roman Road came over Harris End then through Oakenclough and on past Stang Yule, the route followed by the present day road. At the bottom of the hill the old road went straight on, where the grass track now goes, and across the River Brock to Longridge Fell. There is little car parking space in this area, but it is usually possible to leave a car below the wooded area, on

the verge of the steep hill or on the wide verge further south at the road
junction. There is more space to park in Calder Vale which also has an
infrequent bus service.

WALK 35 (Maps 18, 19, 17, 20)   *Calder Vale Hazelhurst, Langden Castle,
Saddle, Wolfen Hall, Wickens Lane End,
Bleasdale, Calder Vale. 26½km or 16½
miles.*

*12kms road, 3½kms with traffic, 2½kms track, 12kms path, most of it fell
walking. A long walk with two climbs, three fords in the Langden valley,
route usually fairly easy except after heavy rain. A compass is essential at
Fiendsdale Head and Saddle. The walk can be shortened by 3km or 2 miles
by parking on the Oakenclough Road.*
By bus: Infrequently to Calder Vale.
*By car: to Calder Vale, by the Methodist Church, approaching from the
Garstang side of the village, or on the Oakenclough road south of Stang
Yule.*

From CALDER VALE

There are two routes from here, both on good tracks. (Map 18).
 From the bridge we keep left around the green up to the terraced houses
of Long Row. The road goes along the front of the terrace and then around
to the right climbing up behind it, but we can cut off this bend by turning
right at the start of the terrace and through a stile up a steep path between
hedges to the track above (100m).
 Up to the right the track bends and becomes a tarred road to farm
buildings (150km).
 We turn right over the cattle grid and along the concrete road then left at
the next cattle grid (120m).
 Up the concrete road we pass a cottage and come between walls to the
gate into Landskill Farm (230m).
 Through the iron gate we keep straight on through the yard onto a firm
track between walls (70m). The track bends left and on again to turn left
then right before the cattle grid (200m).
 Avoiding the cattle grid the track goes up the hill through a gate and
alongside the wall to a gate onto the tarred road (600m).
The alternative route follows the river.
 We keep left around the green, up along the front of the terrace of Long
Row and straight on through a gate on a tarred path by the mill
race (200m).
 Beyond the mill dam the path climbs through woodland to come alongside
the church yard wall (600m).
 Past the school the road comes to a junction and goes left to the
Moorcock but we turn right and into the farmyard on a good track bearing
left alongside trees and through an iron gate onto a track (250m).
 We follow the track with the wall on our right, through a gate then on over
a cattle grid and left up the track, through a gate and alongside the wall to a
gate onto the tarred road (800m).

Photo 71. The Langden Valley at the foot of Fiendsdale.

From OAKENCLOUGH ROAD to FIENDSDALE (Map 18)

To the right the road goes down to Snape Rake but we turn left. We bend left then dip to a slight right hand bend and on the right is a gap in the wall (200m). A narrow path through the conifer plantation comes across grass onto the tarred road beyond (50m).

Turning right around the edge of Fell Plantation and past Fell End Farm we enter woodland at the lodge (1km).

The road is through woodland to a road junction where we turn left (500m). We cross Clough Heads Brook then through Clough Heads Wood on to Hazelhurst Farm (1¼km).

The road goes beyond the farm then right over a cattle grid (250m) (Map 19). Just before the grid we turn left amongst scattered gorse and rushes to go up by the wall and coming between wall and fence to a gate in the wall at the foot of the fell (250m).

Through the gate we turn right to follow the wall (200m).

The wall bends left then right again (150m).

Beyond here the path continues along the wall to a signboard then left up a long straight rake (200m).

From this sign board the Access Area is to the right of the rake and above the wall. The rake is a good path and fairly straight but deteriorates as the fell levels near the top. There are several posts on route but where there is doubt in adverse conditions, a bearing of about 60° should bring us near the sign board at the top (1½km).

This signboard marks the northerly corner of the Access Area which extends over to our right.

FIENDSDALE to LANGDEN CASTLE

Beyond the signboard the path continues vague and the bearing to the start of the Fiendsdale path is 30° (Map 17). Once across the heather and peat to the start of the path, the way is clearer and drops steadily down the left side of Fiendsdale with Fiendsdale Water below on the right to level out at the foot of the valley (1km). *Photo 71.*

Keeping Fiendsdale Water on our right, we cross Langden Brook a little way upstream. It is fordable in boots even after winter rain but can be fairly fast flowing. The path goes forward to cross a small stream and follows the foot of steep land, curving right to meet Langden Brook again, at which point it climbs steeply up above the river (200m).

The path keeps up above the river along the edge of the steep land and is at times rather indistinct through bracken and heather. Soon the roof of the Langden Castle building comes into view (500m).

The path leaves the bracken, crossing a small stream at a small cairn, to join the firm track at a ford (90°) and then goes on to Langden Castle (200m).

LANGDEN CASTLE to SADDLE END (Map 17)

The route now is south up the Bleadale valley which faces Langden Castle. Fording places vary with the winter floods, but it is usually best to ford the Langden Brook about the centre of the Bleadale valley. This keeps us above the confluence with the Bleadale Water, which has to be crossed also. Once across the Langden we should bear left to cross the Bleadale Water and we should find a good path developing a little above river level. These two fords are fairly easy in summer in boots, but in winter may require a few carefully placed stones.

The path up the Bleadale valley keeps above the river which is down on our right. The valley bears left then right. Ignore the path which climbs to the left. A large valley joins in from the right and near the confluence of streams is a cairn wall below the path. This is about 1½km from Langden Castle. From here the stream is soon in a narrow rocky ravine with trees below the path and a little further on a small valley enters from the right with a waterfall and rowan tree (600m).

We are now approaching the head of the valley. The path keeps on the left of the main stream all the way, crossing a few tributaries coming from the left and the valley fades out into open fell (300m).

It is essential now to set an accurate course with the compass and follow it carefully (Map 20). A bearing of 187° will bring us over the ridge, with its remnants of fence posts, and should bring us to the start of the path down Saddle (1km).

This is a hollow path which follows the top edge of the Burnslack valley on our left. It is distinct all the way down until the ridge levels into a flat area (1km). We bear right across this flat land to the start of another track, fairly level at first, then becoming more definite as it steepens to a gate in the wall (500m). The track goes down to Saddle End Farm and we go through a gate and straight down a concrete road between walls (500m).

SADDLE END to BLEASDALE

The road goes down between walls and at the end of the walls we turn right along a strip of beech wood (150m) (Map 20).

Beyond the wood we keep on in the same direction following the fence and stream on our right, towards the farm at the foot of Parlick. The stream turns left but we keep straight by the fence to a stile at the fence junction (250m). Over the stile towards Parlick is a deep clough and a gate at the top of the far slope. We make for this gate, crossing Chipping Brook in the bottom of this clough by a wooden footbridge and up towards the electricity pole to find the gate (250m).

Through the gate we follow the fence on our left, then cross it by a gate to follow along the far side with the fence now on our right, across a culvert to a gate (120m).

Straight on with the fence on our right we keep along the back of a stone building to a wooden gate at the far end of the building (50m).

This gate says 'Private' on the back but this is the right of way and no satisfactory alternative exists at the moment. We turn left along the yard past the farmhouse and straight on over a cattle grid on a good road (50m).

The centre section of this road is not a right of way, but it is an acceptable alternative. The road keeps straight on and meets another track at a cattle grid near the main road (700m).

We turn left to the main road at a corner where we turn right along a quiet road, (Map 19) past a road end, to a sharp left turn (2km).

By path from here, we go through a gate on the right at the bend and follow with the wall on our left going through a gate in the field corner. The wall on our left soon becomes a fence and stream to a stone footbridge (700m).

Across the bridge we make for the tallest tree, an ash tree, crossing a stone culvert at a stream corner to a stile at the road and right, down past Bleasdale Post Office to the estate road on the right (500m).

Alternatively we could keep to the road turning right at a road junction which is Wickens Land End, then on and down past Bleasdale Post Office to the Bleasdale Estate road on the right (1½km).

BLEASDALE to OAKENCLOUGH ROAD (Map 18)

Up and along this road, we ignore the right fork and keep on to the cattle grid at Bleasdale School and turn left (600m).

This is a pleasant road, through woodland at times. It goes straight on past the road junction at Brooks Farm, straight over a cattle grid at another road end and soon enters woodland again to the road which we started along where we keep left (2km).

Past the lodge and Fell End Farm we come alongside Fell Plantation which rises steeply on our right (1km).

As the road straightens to the house at the end, we leave it across grass to a little gate in the wall and the path through the conifers to the road (500m).

Along to the left we follow the wood side until opposite a gap in the woodland is a gate and track to Calder Vale (500m).

OAKENCLOUGH ROAD to CALDER VALE

We follow the track down the wall side to the bottom where there are two ways back (600m).

To the right we go over the cattle grid along a track with the wall on our left, through a gate, then another gate into the farm (200m).

We keep to the right by trees through the farm onto the tarred road just beyond then left at the road junction to the school (250m).

We leave the road at the school, keeping along the left side of the churchyard wall on a tarred path down through woodland and along the side of the mill dam to Calder Vale (600m).

Instead of going over the cattle grid we turn left then right around the corner of the wall.

The firm track goes along towards the farm (200m).

The track bends right between walls into the farmyard and straight on through an iron gate onto a concrete road (70m).

Down the road past the cottage we turn right over a cattle grid (300m).

The concrete continues to another cattle grid and we turn left immediately before the farm buildings onto a tarred road (120m).

Down the road it deteriorates to a firm track and bends right (150m).

Just past the bend an obvious stone stile gap leads steeply down between hedges for a short cut. The track continues down around the end of the terrace (100m).

WALK 36 (Map 18)   *Calder Vale, Moorcock, Oakenclough, Calder Vale.*
6kms or 4 miles.
4kms road, little traffic, 1½kms tracks and metalled paths, ½km on grass. A
short walk around Calder Vale area.
By bus or car: to Calder Vale, parking near the Methodist Church

CALDER VALE to OAKENCLOUGH

We keep left around the green, up along the terraced houses of Long Row
and straight on through a gate on a tarred path by the mill race (200m).
Beyond the dam the path climbs through woodland to the church (600m).
Beyond the school is a junction and we turn left to the Moorcock along the
tarred road (1km).
Along to the left past the Moorcock the road drops to cross the River Calder.
On the right here are the buildings which used to be Oakenclough paper mill
but is now subdivided for use by a number of firms (800m).

OAKENCLOUGH to CALDER VALE

Over the bridge at the road junction we turn left with views across the valley
to a corner where the road turns left (1½km).
Beyond the corner, the road off to the right goes to Barnacre Church but we
keep straight on to a bungalow on the left and a gate just beyond (600m).
Through the iron gate we keep to the right along the side of the field, following
the fence on our right to a stile in the hedge (130m). Straight on with the fence
on our right we cross a footbridge to a stile in the hedge (50m.)
We bear left straight across the field to a stile in the fence and on again to a
footbridge over a ditch onto a good path (200m).
Along the path and straight through a stone stile gap we come onto a narrow
path behind the houses and down steps to the co-op (240m). We can turn left
down the road back to the Methodist Church (170m).
Or cross the road past the co-op and the terrace of houses, but forking right
to keep on the more level road past two other houses and on down the track
through woodland to a good footbridge over the river just before the next
houses (500m).
Across the bridge we follow the river back upstream coming along a path
below woodland and between farm buildings. We keep right of the stone
farmhouses then left along the side of the mill (800m).

WALK 37 (Map 18, 19)   *Snape Rake, River Brock, Jack Anderton's Bridge,*
Bleasdale Church, Hazelhurst, Stang Yule, Snape
Rake. 10km or 6 miles.
6km road, little or no traffic. 4km of field and riverside paths, fairly dry. Or a
short walk of 5km with 2km of road. Beautiful riverside, woodland and
upland pasture.
By car: On the Oakenclough to Bleasdale road on the steep hill beyond the
woodland there are one or two parking places, or at the bottom of the hill on
a wide verge at the gate to Snape Rake.
By bus: To Calder Vale and an extra 3km walk described on page 116 "From
Calder Vale".

From SNAPE RAKE along the RIVER BROCK (Map 18)

At the road junction, opposite the Oakenclough road, we go through a wooden gate and follow the route of the Roman Road along a grass track through an avenue of pine trees to a stile at a wooden gate in a fence (300m). A firm track goes steeply down through woodland to a good footbridge over the River Brock (200m) *Photo 70 (page 115)*.

This is beautiful woodland particularly the autumn beeches and upstream is even better. Over the bridge the path forks, the left fork following the river.

> This is an undulating rough path which is well used but not really a right of way as yet (200m).
>
> The path levels on grass close to the river bank, and follows the river to a small fenced field which is the Scout Camp (300m).

The right fork is the drier route in wet conditions. It climbs only to drop again, but it is a right of way. For a short way it follows the route of the Roman Road.

> We bear right up a hollow track to the tarred road (170m).
>
> On along the road by the wood side, the road bends where the wood on our left ends, and at a bridleway signpost a rough track goes left between stone gate posts (300m).
>
> Down the hollow track it deteriorates at a clough and doubles back down to the left, improving slightly as it levels and bends right again. We make straight for the river past two beech trees (300m) (Map 18 again).
>
> We turn right close along the riverside to a small fenced field which is the Scout Camp (120m).

We ignore the inviting stile and keep around the outside of the camp along the riverside path (120m).

Keeping close to the river all the way, the path leaves woodland and goes over a stile at a fence corner into riverside pasture (300m).

We follow the riverside fence on our left to the ruins of Gill Barn and a good wooden footbridge (400m).

Here the Brock divides with paths following both branches but we go over the bridge with the river on our left, follow the fence to a sharp corner and then steeply up by woodland (200m).

Just a few metres before the top we go over a simple stile on our left to follow with the fence on our right at the top of steep woodland on a good path except for a minor detour by a fence junction to cross a gully (150m).

Along again in the wood with the fence on our right, on a good path with oak and beech sloping steeply to the river below, we see a glimpse of the road on our left at Jack Anderton's Bridge, but we keep up along the top of the wood to a stile at the road (250m).

> The short walk turns left down over the bridge and steeply up again then level all the way back past the lodge, a double bend at Tootle Hall and on to the junction at Snape Rake (2km). We turn right up the hill (1km).
>
> For Calder Vale, up again alongside the woodland onto the level and a gated track on the left opposite a gap in the woodland (800m).
>
> Described from here on page 120 "Oakenclough Road to Calder Vale".

For the longer walk we bear right up the hill to the farm on the left (30m). Turning into the farm road we go straight on to just past the first building on

the right, and turn right before the large modern building to go along a track between wall and fence to a gate at the end (130m).
Through the gate into the field we bear slightly right, with the fence on our left, on past the fence corner to a wooden gate in the field corner (360m).
To avoid the farm we keep along the road which soon drops steeply. Here the Bleasdale estate road on our left leads straight to a cattle grid at the school where we can turn left, or straight on to the church (1½km).

Through BLEASDALE

There are two routes from here. The first on roads is 2km shorter.
We turn left along the road crossing a stream to enter woodland (400m).
The road goes through the wood then another short piece of woodland and across the River Brock to Brooks Farm (400m).
We keep straight on at the junction then over a cattle grid at another junction keeping straight on to enter woodland again (400m).
The road goes on through the wood to buildings at a road junction (300m).
Bearing left in woodland again the road passes the lodge (500m).
The longer route is by road and path past Bleasdale Church (Map 19).
We turn right along the road then left at the junction past school and church on over a cattle grid (500m).
We follow the road on under trees past Vicarage Farm (450m).
The road goes on towards Admarsh Barn Farm where it turns left to the farm gate (400m).
Through the gate we turn immediately right off the road along side the fence keeping behind the modern building on a narrow path to a stile at the far end and straight on along the fence side of a short field to a gate (100m).
Through the gate we follow the grass track with the fence on our right across a small stream then a larger stream, which is the River Brock, by footbridges (300m).
Straight on again with the hedge on our right we cross a fence by a stile and on again through a gate onto the road at a cattle grid (450m).
We turn left along the road past Hazelhurst Farm (300m) (Map 18).
It goes on past Clough Heads Wood to cross Clough Heads Brook (1km).
We go on past all the farm buildings to the junction at the end where we turn right into woodland again (300m).
The road keeps on through woodland past the lodge (500m).
We follow the road by more woodland past Fell End Farm (500m).
Fell Plantation rises up from the roadside on our right, and the road curves round it, then as it straightens towards the house at the end, we leave the road across grass to a small gate in the wall on our left (500m).
A narrow path leads through the plantation to the road (50m).
Along to the left the road follows the wood side, and opposite a gap in the wood is a gate and track to Calder Vale (200m).
Straight on to the bottom is the junction at Snape Rake (2km).

OAKENCLOUGH ROAD to CALDER VALE is on page 120

MAP 19 FAIRSNAPE

Everyone who knows the Chipping area knows Parlick. From the south it stands forward of its neighbours, steep, symmetrical and conical in shape. It is readily recognisable from all sides which makes it an obvious landmark. It is just steep enough and high enough to offer a challenge. When you get to the top there is a wonderful view which makes it all worth the effort. On a breezy day there are often a few hang-gliders soaring around the top of the fell, taking advantage of the strong air currents which blow up the steep smooth slope of the fell. North east over Saddle is the high ridge of Totridge which drops steeply to the green fields of Little Bowland. To the southeast is the broad extent of Longridge Fell with Chipping in the foreground. Most of the Lancashire coast can be seen from the top of Parlick, and further still from Fairsnape a little way to the north. It is an easy grassy walk to Fairsnape, but rather less so down to Fiendsdale Head. To the east along the top of the ridge it is mostly rough peat haggs and wet sphagnum moss.

Steeply down at the foot of Fairsnape are the scattered farms of the Bleasdale Estate. The estate is centred around the large victorian house called Bleasdale Tower, but the hamlet of Bleasdale is usually thought of as the church, the buildings around the school and perhaps the post office cafe. People have lived in these parts since prehistoric times. Early bronze age settlers built a circle of wooden posts here in about 1800 BC. We don't know for certain why they built it but it must have been a very important place. To us it is just Bleasdale Circle.

Fairsnape and the west side of Parlick are now part of the access area which extends over to Burnslack. Walkers can ramble freely over access areas

Photo 72. Fairsnape and Parlick from Bleasdale.

provided the bylaws are observed, no dogs and no fires or stoves. There are several convenient access points to the fells and the directions link these together for those who wish to go up one way and down another.

The most convenient access point is Fell Foot where there is space to park a few cars, or on the road to the west which has a wide verge. There are better parking facilities in Chipping which is also the nearest bus route. A compass is required on the fell tops especially in doubtful weather.

The directions for maps 19 & 20 link together the access points of the access areas.

WALK 38   *Chipping, Fell Foot, Blindhurst Fell, Hazelhurst,*
(Maps 20, 19, 18)   *Bleasdale, Chipping. 15km or 9 miles.*
10½km of roads with little traffic, 4km of it without any, 1km tracks, 3½km field paths or on grass. This walk links together the access points onto the fells for those who wish to walk the fell tops. It is an enjoyable walk around the fell bottom and through the Bleasdale Estate with some woodland. A compass would be a great help along the fell bottom, but not essential.
By bus or car: to Chipping village.
By car: to Fell Foot where there is space for a few cars at the bottom of the lane at the corner.

UP from CHIPPING to FELL FOOT (Map 20)

We leave Chipping by the road which goes up round the corner of the churchyard and by Church Rake towards the fells (300m).

A road dips to the right but we keep level along to the left (700m).

The road becomes narrow through trees and dips to cross a stream then on to the road junction at Fish House (550m).

We turn left and soon climb steeply to another junction (500m).

Here we turn right on a level road to a corner where a track goes straight on up (500m).

> The track goes to Fell Foot at the foot of Parlick Access Area (400m). Most walkers go straight up to the top keeping to the left of the clough but there are easier ways which start along the fell bottom to the left and wind their way up more slowly. (Map 19).

FELL FOOT to BLINDHURST FELL (Map 19)

Just at the bottom of the track near the road, opposite a cattle grid, is a footpath with signpost, stile and gate which keeps around the bottom of Parlick and Fairsnape then up to Hazelhurst for Fiendsdale. Over the stile we bear right across the field (283°) keeping well to the left of two thorns to a stile in the wall (240m).

Over the stile and straight ahead we make for the right hand end of trees on the near skyline (292°) crossing shallow cloughs to a stile in the wall (350m). Over the stile and straight on again (308°) we come to steps in the wall (150m).

Over the steps and keeping in the same direction roughly parallel to the fell bottom (305°) we cross a small stream and on to a strong stream in a clough at a fence junction (300m).

We go down across the stream and over a stile then keeping along with the fence on our right we go over a stile into the Access Area at a signboard (30m). This is Blindhurst Fell bottom.

BLINDHURST FELL to HAZELHURST (Map 19)

We keep left along the side of the fence to a gate where we leave the Access Area again (150m).

Straight on with the fence and hedge on our left, we dip to a junction of tracks near a gate (200m).

Ignoring the gate we keep to the near side of the hedge again, following the lower of two tracks which soon bears right and down the fell to a thorn tree where it meets the lower track along the fence side (160m).

There is a poor stile over the fence and we go down across the field to ford a stream at a fence corner (100m).

We bear left on a track which fades out but we follow the fence on our left to the corner then straight on to go through the left hand end of a small wood, and ford a stream to a wooden gate in the fence (350m).

On towards the farm buildings of Higher Fairsnape we follow the fence on our left, then going through a gate in the fence we continue along with the fence now on our right, along a grass track to an iron gate in the wall (250m).

Along the track again straight all the way, we go through the left gate in the wire fence, with the hedge on our right, on along the track again to a gate onto the road (450m).

This is Higher Fairsnape and there are two farms here.

We turn right through the gate in the wall, keep around the end of the stone building on our left and along the firm track to a gate in a wall (200m).

We go through the gate and bear right around the buildings, through a gate at the corner, and straight on along a track with a fence on our left to a gate (200m).

Straight through the gate we have the fence on our left again, then straight on by the ditch with the wall further away on our left, to a gate at the far end of the wall (600m).

We go through the gate and across a culvert to follow a fence on our right to a firm track (100m).

To the left the track becomes a right of way after the first 400m and is then a tarred road past church and school to Bleasdale Post Office (2km).

We turn right along the track, by trees and through a gate (150m).

The track crosses a stream, which is the River Brock, on to Holme House Farm (250m).

We go straight through the farm by two gates onto a firm track, with the back of the farmhouse on our left, and along the track we bend right and then up over the cattle grid at the corner (225m).

The track goes on to Hazelhurst (300m).

For FIENDSDALE

We turn right at the cattle grid through scattered gorse and rushes through a gate in the wall and turn right along the fell bottom as described on page 118. This is the northern end of the Access Area.

HAZELHURST to BLEASDALE POST OFFICE (Map 18)

The road goes straight through at Hazelhurst Farm and on through Clough Heads Wood to cross Clough Heads Brook (1km).

We pass all the buildings to the junction at the end where we turn left (300m). The road soon bears right but we go over a cattle grid straight on by Brooks Farm (700m).

On through woodland at times the road goes on to a junction at the school (1km).

We turn right here to the main road and left by Bleasdale Post Office (700m).

BLEASDALE POST OFFICE to CHIPPING (Maps 19, 20)

It is mostly a road walk back to Chipping. Up the hill to Wickens Lane End where we turn left and along past a road end to a sharp bend left then right again (1½km).

Some of this road can be avoided by a field path. Up the hill from Bleasdale Post Office the road levels out and on the left opposite an ash tree the fence steps back a little and just beyond we go over a stile (150m).

We cross a rushy field towards the lower one of two farms to find a stone culvert at a stream corner, then on again in the same direction to cross a stone footbridge (500m).

We follow the stream to the right around a large field to come alongside a wall, through a gate and straight on alongside the wall again on our right, to a gate onto the road at a corner where we turn left (700m).

From here it is straight on past another road end to the bottom of the Fell Foot track (2km).

We turn right then left and steeply down, then right again at Fish House back to Chipping Church (2½km).

Photo 73. Brabin's School.

MAP 20 CHIPPING

Blindhurst, Fairsnape, Wolf Fell and Saddle are now an access area. By agreement with the owners, this land is open for general rambling provided the byelaws are observed. This means principally, no dogs and no fires or stoves.

There are good views from this high land. Eastwards is Waddington Fell, the Hodder valley and in the foreground the green, limestone countryside of Little Bowland. To the south east is the broad extent of Longridge Fell. Most of the summit ridge from Fairsnape to Totridge is a maze of peat haggs which makes it difficult walking along the tops. Fairsnape, Parlick and Saddle are fairly easy walking but Wolf Fell is mostly rocky.

Below Wolf Fell is Chipping Brook which provided water power for local industry. There were seven mills in Chipping, now there is only one. Berry's Chair Works was a water powered cotton mill until the end of the 1860's. It is now quite a large thriving factory but it still retains its original character. This group of old stone buildings and the little stone bridge at a bend of the brook are particularly attractive. Another old mill was the local corn mill in the village. The mill wheel has now been restored and is in working order again, and the old mill building is now a restaurant.

Chipping really is a delightful village with 17th and 18th century stone houses, narrow streets and cobbled yards, village shops and village pubs. One of the oldest houses in the village is the post office. Chipping's 17th century benefactor John Brabin lived there. He died in 1683 and in his will established a charity which brought into being the almshouses and Brabin's School. St Bartholomew's Church was rebuilt in the 16th century on the site of a much earlier church probably earlier than the 11th century. There is a very old yew tree in the church yard and a sundial. St Mary's Catholic Church of 1828 is outwardly very plain but by contrast has a very decorative interior. The United Reformed Church was built in 1838 but there were nonconformists in the Chipping area long before that. Chipping comes from the Old English word for barter. Being just outside the Forest of Bowland at a convenient crossing place of the Chipping Brook, it would be a natural place for a market to develop for the cattle and diary produce of Bowland.

The bus service runs from Preston to Chipping and occasionally to Clitheroe. There is ample car parking space in the village car park, off the Garstang road by the village hall, and there is space for just a few cars at Fell Foot below Parlick.

The directions for maps 19 and 20 link together the access points of the access area, for those who wish to go up from one point and down to another. A compass is required on the fell tops especially in doubtful weather.

WALK 39 (Maps 19, 20) *Chipping, Fish House, Fell Foot, Wolfen Hall, Chipping. 5½kms or 3½ miles.*
4kms on roads with little traffic, 1½kms on farm roads and firm tracks. A dry easy walk up the Chipping valley to the fell bottom and back.
By bus or car: to Chipping village.

CHIPPING to FISH HOUSE

We leave Chipping by the road which goes up around the corner of the churchyard and by Church Rake towards the fells (300m).

A road dips to the right and we shall come back this way. Keeping left we pass the neat row of cottages called Old Hive and along to a bend at Top 'o Saunder where the road drops steeply to cross a stream (800m).

Up a little and along to Fish House where we turn left (450m).

The road to the right here leads steeply down to buildings which were once Wolfen Mill, later a dairy and now a house, and on to a small stone bridge over Chipping Brook, which we cross on the way back.

FISH HOUSE to FELL FOOT

Along to the left we soon start to climb, then more steeply before abruptly levelling out along to a road junction. The road to the left leads to Beacon Fell Country Park but we turn right here (500m).

It is level along to the corner of the road where we keep straight on to a cattle grid on the right where we turn off (500m).

The track leads up to Fell Foot (400m).

FELL FOOT to WOLFEN MILL

Over the cattle grid we go along the farm road. The centre portion of this road is not a right of way but is an acceptable alternative. We come to Wolfen

Hall through a tall stone gateway and immediately right through a similar stone gateway to leave the farmhouse behind us (700m).

The track leads down towards Wolfen Mill, bending left then right to pass a house and on to the tarred road where we turn left over the little stone bridge across Chipping Brook (800m).

WOLFEN MILL to CHIPPING

Steeply up from the bridge we come to a junction and turn right (100m).

The road is fairly level for a while, then goes down hill, then steeply down Tweedy Brow. On the right here was Tweedy's Brass Foundry and a row of cottages now all demolished (500m).

The road is level along by Chipping Brook and the mill pond, then drops round by the chair works and over the bridge, then straight on to the church (1km).

WALK 40 (Map 20, 21)   *Chipping, Chipping Laund, Lickhurst, Jenny Hey, Chipping. 8kms or 5 miles.*

2km road with little traffic, 4km firm tracks, 2km mostly dry on grass. In wet weather all but 200m of this walk can be on firm track and road. Easy walking in pasture, some woodland, and along the foot of the fells with no climbing.

By bus or car: to Chipping.

We leave Chipping down Talbot Street and over Chipping Brook then left at the war memorial on the Little Bowland and Leagram road (200m), (Map 20).

We keep along the road past the old lodge house and turn left over a cattle grid at the footpath guide post 'Stanley 1½' (550m).

Along the tarred road, bending right along the end of the wood we bear right at the fork of the road and go alongside the fence to Chipping Laund (700m).

We bear left at the entrance, following the firm track past the farm and over the cattle grid (100m).

There are two routes from here, the first a bit wet at times past the end of the wood but otherwise dry, the second keeps along the road.

We leave the track, crossing to the right of woodland through rushes and right of a row of thorn trees to go along an old bank to a stile under a tree at the end of the wall (450m) (Map 21).

Over the stile in the same direction as before, we go across the field towards the lowest part of the wood, down over a stile in the fence and left down by the top of the woodland to a footbridge (150m).

This is a good wooden bridge over Leagram Brook and across it we go round to the right and steeply up to cross the level field towards buildings in the trees, and a stile in the fence by an electricity pole (250m).

On in the same direction we go through a stone gateway and turn right past the farmhouse (120m).

For wet weather we can keep to the track from Chipping Laund (Map 20).
Following the firm track we turn right at a junction and on along the track
towards Park Gate, dropping down to cross Leagram Brook by a stone
bridge (800m).
Through the gate we turn right up to the house at Park Gate, keeping
right, straight along the front of the house and straight through the
wooden gate by the wood into the field (150m) (Map 21).
We turn left along the hedge side, through a gate and straight on with the
fence on our right (200m) (Map 21).
On our right a gate leads onto a good dry track which is level to a bend
then drops to the old farmhouse at Park Style (250m).
At the farm buildings we keep right along the front of the old farmhouse, bear
left at the end of the building past a trough, and on through trees on a fair
track (150m).
Straight on through a gate the track is rough with a fence on our right. The
track turns through a gate on our right onto a good track (80m).
We follow the firm track down to cross a culvert and through a gate (170m).
Following the track towards farm buildings we go through a gate (300m).
This gate has a private road notice on the back which refers to vehicles.
Through a gate is a junction in the track. To the right goes past Lickhurst to
Burholme Bridge, but we turn left at the junction and follow the track with the
stream over to our right, to a left hand bend (700m).
On again along the track we are on a low hill called Stanley, then we go down
to a ford and gate (650m) (Map 20).
On along the track we pass Jenny Hey Barn on our left then left at a junction
onto a good tarred road to a gate (750m).
Through the gate the road has a stream alongside on the right, then the
stream goes under the road and we come past a bend to gates opposite each
other. Saddle to the right, Windy Hills to the left (750m).
The footpath route to Chipping turns left along the Windy Hills track and
is described on page 137 "Down from Saddle End to Chipping by path".
For the road route we keep on along the road past Bradley Barn down to a
road junction (650m).
A road goes steeply down to the right but we keep level along to the left. The
road is level at first then downhill then drops steeply to a factory and is level
again along by the mill pond (1km).
We follow the road past the chair works and over the bridge then up slightly
to meet another road, and straight on to the church (500m).

Photo 74. Parlick, Wolf Fell and Saddle from the road to Doeford Bridge.

WALK 41 (Maps 20, 17, 19) *Chipping, Windy Hills, Saddle, Langden Castle, Fiendsdale, Holme House, Fell Foot, Chipping. 18½kms or 11½ miles.*
3km road with little traffic, 3½km firm tracks, 6km fell walking, some of it on fell paths, 6km lowland paths and fields.
A long walk with two climbs, three fords in the Langden valley, route usually fairly dry except after heavy rain. A compass is essential at Fiendsdale Head and Saddle. Don't be disappointed, there is no castle at Langden Castle. By bus or car: to Chipping village.

UP from CHIPPING to SADDLE FELL by path

(Map 20 2½kms or 1½ miles.)
We leave Chipping by the road which goes up round the corner of the churchyard and on by Church Rake towards the fells (300m).
A road bears left but we dip to the right following the road over the bridge, past Berry's Chair Works, to the mill pond above (200m).
Halfway along the pond a track bears right just beyond a bungalow, and we go over a stile in the fence just at the start of this track, by a signpost, keeping steeply up to the right to an electricity pole at the top of the hill (50m).
We bear left here following up with the thorn hedge on our right to the top of the rise (160m).
Straight on at the field corner with the thorn hedge still on our right, we come to a good stile in a fence (90m).

We keep straight on again along a hollow path past an electricity pole. The hollow path drops left past an ash tree but we leave it to keep slightly higher up the field to come level along to a stile in the fence (400m).

Over the stile we keep level along above the nearer trees (10°) then drop left to cross a good footbridge. It can be slippery in wet weather (150m).

Over the footbridge we follow the edge of the field with Dobson's Brook on our left to come onto the farm track (200m).

Left along the track we cross the bridge then up beneath trees and level along to a wooden gate onto the tarred road (300m).

We go straight across through a wooden gate onto a concrete road which goes on and up to Saddle End Farm (300m).

We come between walls to the farm, keeping straight on through gates with a stone building on our left, out to the field beyond (100m).

Straight on from the farm on a firm track we follow the wall on our left until it ends, then keeping along a left fork on a rougher track we go over a stile at a gate in the fence (350m).

On up the track we go through a gate in the wall into the Access Area (250m).

SADDLE FELL to LANGDEN CASTLE

A good but rough track goes up from the gate with good views down into the valley and across to Wolf Fell on the left. The track levels then climbs slightly and deteriorates (500m).

There is a flat portion of fell here before it starts to rise again and we cross to the right to come into sight of the Burnslack valley (150m).

We keep up along the top of the steep valley side and very soon a hollow path developes which keeps close to the edge of the steep land with good views down onto the valley floor. It is essential that we follow this track for the best crossing of the ridge ahead. The path becomes less steep at the top and takes a distinct bend round to the left away from the valley side. At the start of this bend we leave the path and set a compass course of 7° which we must follow carefully (800m).

The top of the ridge from Fairshape to Totridge is a maze of peat haggs and by following this bearing we cross at the easiest place.

Along the flat top there used to be a long straight fence marking the county boundary. Now there are just a few posts. It is 1km across the ridge to the Bleadale path and the fence is half way.

The path down Bleadale follows the right bank of Bleadale Water so the important thing here is to keep going downstream with the water always on our left. Even if we are on the wrong tributary we must eventually get it right. If we have deviated too far to the left in crossing the ridge, we shall be following a main tributary in a definite valley with no path, heading for a rowan tree and a waterfall. If this happens it is better to get over to the right into the main valley before we get too far down. The path once we find it follows the Bleadale Water all the way, generally keeping somewhat above the valley floor. The waterfall and rowan tree is over to our left (300m).

The path keeps above a few trees in a rocky ravine, and just beyond, a wide valley joins from the left (500m).

There is a cairn down in the valley where the rivers meet and the valley soon bends left then right to a view of the stone building called Langden Castle (1½km).

The path fades out as we near the Langden Brook and we keep heading to the right of Langden Castle for the easiest crossing of the Bleadale Water, then head for the building for the crossing of the Langden Brook and on to the track at Langden Castle (250m).

In summer there should be no great difficulty crossing these rivers in boots, but after heavy rain a few carefully placed stones may be required.

Photo 75. The route upstream from Langden Castle.   *Photo 76. The Langden Valley towards Fiendsdale.*

LANGDEN CASTLE to FIENDSDALE HEAD (Map 17)

We turn left at Langden Castle and follow the track which is a right of way to the first ford and here we leave it almost due west (270°) in the direction of the notch in the skyline where the far end of the track turns the fell end. *Photo 75.* This leads to a small cairn below a patch of heather (200m).

Crossing the stream, the good path through bracken soon becomes indistinct but we keep to the top of the steep slope above the river, eventually dropping to river level just before the Fiendsdale valley on the left, *photo 76* (500m).

The path crosses Langden Brook upstream of Fiendsdale Water. It is fordable in boots even after winter rain but it is nevertheless fairly fast flowing (200m).

The path climbs steadily through heather along the steep side of the valley with Fiendsdale Water below on the left, and as it levels to Fiendsdale Head the path fades out. A signboard ahead (210°) marks the route (1km).

The signboard is at the northerly corner of the Access Area, and a path is waymarked over towards Fairsnape Fell on the left, starting about 100m before the sign, for those who wish to follow the ridge along to Fell Foot. Whilst this part of the walk is easy enough on a sunny day, in bad weather the short portion across by the post is a likely place to get lost. Even a few metres off the path and it is hard to imagine it is there at all.

Beyond the signboard the path is still vague but a bearing of 239° for about 150m should bring us to the start of the path down Holme House Fell.

DOWN from FIENDSDALE to BLINDHURST FELL
(Map 19)

From the signboard a bearing of 239° leads to a more definite path as the fell steepens. A long straight rake goes down Holme House Fell to come alongside the wall at a signboard near a gate (1½km).

Ignoring the gate we follow the wall which bends left then right again at a wall junction (250m).

We follow the wall again and leave the fell by a wooden gate on the left (200m). We go down through rushes and scattered gorse between fence and wall to meet the road where we turn left over a cattle grid (250m).

We follow the track down turning left to the farm along the back of the farmhouse at Holme House Farm (210m).

Straight through two gates the track deteriorates somewhat to cross a stream which is the River Brock and goes on bending right to follow the wall by trees to a gate (265m).

Through the gate the wall bends out in a large recess. We follow the track by the fence side and where the fence turns left we leave the track and follow the fence side to go over a culvert and through a gate at the wall (250m).

Straight on along the side of the ditch towards the top of Parlick, we come close to the wall at a few small trees and keep straight on between ditch and fence to a gate (600m).

Through the gate we follow the track along the fence on our right to farm buildings, going through a gate at the corner and keeping on around the corner of the building we cross to a gate in the wall (200m.) This is Higher Fairsnape. Through the gate a firm track leads towards the farm houses and we turn right at a stone building on our right to follow the track down past a trough and straight through a gate down the road (130m).

Along the road the wall on our left becomes a fence and we turn left off the road through a gate at the first fence junction (70m).

We follow with the fence on our left through a gate then on again with the fence on our left on a grass track to a gate in the wall (450m).

We keep straight on following the fence towards woodland and near the end we turn left through a gate in the fence to cross to another gate in the small wood (250m).

We bear right to ford a stream and cross the field (170°) towards the lowest shoulder of fell above trees to come alongside a fence on our right on a vague track (350m).

The track fords a steam at the corner and we go straight across the narrow field up to the fence and a poor stile (100m).

A track keeps level along the far side of the fence but we cross it and behind a thorn tree we take the track which inclines up the fell to the right to meet other tracks near a gate (160m).

Ignoring the gate we keep straight on parallel to the hedge on our right. A little way above the gate an obvious hollow track leads up the fell but we keep to the right parallel to the hedge, becoming level along to a gate into the Access Area (200m). This is Blindhurst Fell.

DOWN from BLINDHURST FELL to FELL FOOT

We keep along with the fence on our right. The fence dips to a stream and just before it at a signboard we cross the fence by a stile on the right (150m). Following the fence round to the left we come to another stile (30m).

We go down to cross the stream and up with the fence on our left. On the level above the stream we leave the fence keeping roughly parallel to the fell bottom (125°) towards the point where the left end of Longridge Fell meets the near skyline, and crossing a stream in a shallow clough, come to steps in the wall (300m).

Keeping along the lower part of the field we come to a stile in the wall to the left of trees (128°) (150m).

From the stile we make towards the end of Longridge Fell (112°) crossing a stream in a rushy clough and straight past the end of a wall on our right to a stile in the wall ahead, to the right of thorn trees (350m).

Over the stile we keep straight on along an old bank towards Pendle Hill (103°) to meet the Fell Foot track at a gate and stile with a footpath signpost (240m) (Map 20).

We turn right for Chipping.

DOWN from FELL FOOT to CHIPPING (Map 20)

The track down from Fell Foot meets the road at a corner and we keep straight on to turn left at the next junction (500m).

We soon drop steeply then up slightly to a road junction at Fish House where we turn right (500m).

The road soon becomes narrow through trees and dips to cross a stream (550m).

Beyond the trees the road is fairly level past cottages at Old Hive to a junction (700m).

We bear right along to the church and the village (300m).

WALK 42 (Map 20)   *Chipping, Burnslack, Saddle End, Chipping.*
                 7¼km or 4½ miles.
4km of quiet roads with little traffic, 1¼km tracks, 2km paths.
A short walk along the fell bottom and back through fields. Usually a dry walk.
By bus or car: to Chipping village.

UP from CHIPPING to BURNSLACK by road

We leave Chipping by the road which goes up around the churchyard and by Church Rake towards the fells (300m).

Where the road forks, we dip to the right following the road over the bridge past Berry's Chair Works and the mill pond above (200m).

The road is level along by Chipping Brook but beyond the factory building it climbs steeply, then less steeply, then levels again to a junction (1km).

A road goes very steeply down to our left but we keep straight on then up to pass Bradley Barn and level again (1km).

We come alongside a stream on our left to a gate onto open fell. The tarred road continues to a junction (500m).

To the right a rough track goes past Jenny Hey Barn, but we bear left on a better track up past woodland, then levelling out over two cattle grids to Burnslack (800m).

Past the front of the house and round the corner we come between walls to the fell gate and the Access Area notice board. The Access Area extends from the valley bottom westward over Saddle. The fells to the right of this valley are not included.

BURNSLACK to SADDLE END

We keep up the wall side to another Access Area sign board and turn left through a gate (150m).

We follow the wall on our left between the ruins of Ward's End and keep along the fell bottom with the fence on our left past a stone barn (200m).

The rough path goes alongside a wall then in the open again past a trough and the remains of Saddle Side (250m).

Down a hollow path we go on to Saddle End Farm and a gate on our left (500m).

DOWN from SADDLE END to CHIPPING by path

Through the gate at Saddle End Farm we come onto a concrete road which goes straight through alongside farm buildings, down between walls and levels out to the main road at a gate (400m).

Straight across the road is another wooden gate and a firm track to Windy Hills. We follow the track along then down beneath trees to a bridge over Dobson's Brook (300m).

The track goes up to Windy Hills but just over the bridge we leave it, turning right into the field and following Dobson's Brook along to a good footbridge (200m).

The bridge can be rather slippery in wet weather. Over it we bear right on a vague path past an oak tree and up to the field where we turn right at a tall ash tree to come level above the trees along to a stile in the fence (150m).

Over the stile we keep level to come left of a tall ash tree (198°) and join a hollow path along to an electricity pole and beyond it a stile in the fence (400m).

Over the stile we keep straight on with the hedge on our left, and straight on again at the field corner with the hedge still on our left to an electricity pole and then steeply down to the right to a footpath guide post and stile and in the fence onto the road (300m).

We turn left along the side of the mill pond and down the road past the chair works (200m).

The road rises slightly to a junction and we go straight on to the church (300m).

WALK 43   *Chipping, Gibbon Bridge, Greystoneley,*
(Maps 20, 21, 16, 17)   *Dinkling Green, Hareden, Langden Castle,*
                                   Saddle, Chipping. 23km or 14 miles.
8km road, about 4km of with some traffic, 7½km tracks, 7½km paths,
mostly fell paths. A long walk through lovely country, some riverside,
woodland and fell. Two fords at Langden Castle followed by a climb over
Saddle. A compass is essential on Saddle. The walk can be shortened by
taxi or a second car. From the telephone box at Greystoneley it is 14km or 9
miles, for instance.
By bus or car: to Chipping village.

CHIPPING to LOUD MYTHOM then LOUD MYTHOM to GREYSTONELEY

We follow the directions from page 144.

GREYSTONELEY to HAREDEN

Opposite the telephone box at Greystoneley is a gate to a farm track and we follow this track over cattle grids then down to Dinkling Green Farm (Map 16) (1km).

At the farm, the track leads between two buildings, the one on our right having a small brick addition, and in the yard we turn immediately right to a field gate at the end of the buildings (60m). *Photo 64 and 65 page 108.*

Due north across the field is a simple stile and across the corner of the next field another similar stile (250m).

Left along a narrow field with the hedge on our left we meet a good track (200m). Turning right we cross a stream, through the farmyard at Higher Fence Wood, and up to the road junction (250m).

Left along the road we dip over a stream and as the road turns left, we climb to the right to enter a conifer plantation at a gate (500m).

Through the wood we keep to the left fork, and again further on, we keep fairly level on a grass path to a wooden hurdle at the end (500m).

Over the gate we follow a track above beech trees with fell on our left, then down more steeply through trees (300m).

The track can be wet at times in the dip but becomes dry as it climbs to the left on an old track to a gate at the wall corner by a larch tree (200m).

This portion of the walk is under trees and does not come out into the fields below. There is no right of way past New Hey Farm. Through the gate we follow the wall on our right past a pine tree by a small stream then further on by a vague track we bear slightly left to a field gate in the wall ahead (300m).

Through the gate we make for the left side of Mellor Knoll which is the round hill ahead on the right (42°). This is level walking on grass but no track until we get near to Mellor Knoll where the track leads around the end of a row of trees below, to a gate at a wall junction (500m).

We follow the track with the wall on our left. It fades but we keep along the wall side and through a gate to continue along the far side of the wall (600m).

As the slope gets steeper we see Hareden Cottage, a detached stone house, in the valley bottom. We make for the field gate to the right of the house, and over a flat concrete bridge across Hareden Brook (200m).

We follow the road along to the right past the buildings of Hareden Farm, crossing the brook again by a stone bridge on the right (100m).

Across the bridge we keep left alongside the stream following the road out and across the iron bridge over Langden Brook onto the Trough road (300m).

HAREDEN to LANGDEN CASTLE

From the iron bridge over Langden Brook we turn left up the road past Smelt Mill Cottages and on to the conifer plantation at the foot of the Langden valley (1¼)km. (Map 17).

Through the water works entrance gate we go along the driveway under trees to the waterworks house (400m).

Keeping right around the garden railings we go up the track alongside the railings to a good stile at a gate (200m).

The track follows the valley bottom to a rowan tree at Mere Clough (700m). Here a short sharp rise carries the track above the valley floor before it levels and goes on to a fork (100m).

We take the lower route above the river then bending right towards the rock pinnacles of Holdron Castle on the fell above us (1km).

The track goes down to Langden Castle, a stone building which is certainly not a castle (500m).

Here we turn left off the track and up the Bleadale valley to the south.

LANGDEN CASTLE to SADDLE END directions on page 118.

SADDLE END to CHIPPING

We follow the concrete road down to meet the tarred road (400m).

We can return to Chipping along the road, turning right along past Bradley Barn to a junction (600m).

A road goes steeply down but we keep level straight on. The road goes down hill then steeply down, levelling along side Chipping Brook to the mill pond (1km).

Down past the chair works, over the bridge and up to a junction, we go straight on to the church (500m).

Alternatively there is the field route by Windy Hills which is described on page 137 'Down from Saddle End to Chipping by path'.

Photo 77. Whitewell Hotel.

MAP 21 LITTLE BOWLAND

Here the River Hodder is at its best. From the little hamlet of Whitewell it sweeps around the foot of New Laund Hill below the Fairy Holes, through its deep wooded gorge to pasture and woodland beyond. Then swiftly through the stepping stones at Stakes and past Loud Mythom, where the River Loud joins in to flow under Doeford Bridge towards the Ribble. West of the river are the small limestone knolls, green pastures and scattered woodland of Little Bowland and the village of Chipping.

Public transport runs from Clitheroe and Slaidburn to Whitewell and from Preston to Chipping and occasionally from Clitheroe to Chipping.

There is a large car park by the village hall in Chipping and a few roadside parking places between Middle Lees and Whitewell.

WALK 44 (Map 21, 16) *Middle Lees, Whitewell, Burholme Bridge, Fair Oak, Greystoneley, Stakes, Doeford Bridge, Middle Lees. 11km or 7 miles.*

3km road with some traffic. 2½km firm track. 5½km dry walking on grass. A varied walk by riverside, woodland and pasture.

By car: on the Doeford Bridge to Whitewell road, beyond the Cow Ark road end at Middle Lees, is a layby 400m on the right (Map 22), or a wide verge 1km along of the left where the wood meets the road, or at Burholme Bridge (Map 21).

By bus: to Burholme Bridge, or Whitewell and walk along the road to Burholme Bridge.

MIDDLE LEES to BURHOLME BRIDGE via
WHITEWELL (Map 21).

We walk towards Whitewell to an iron gate on the right where the wood meets the road at the alternative parking place (600m). There are two routes from here, the first along the road.

Along the road (Map 16) is a beautiful walk through woodland, some traffic but quiet enough mid week. We keep along past Whitewell Hotel, and on by the river on the Dunsop Bridge road to Burholme Bridge where we turn left (3km).

Avoiding the road with wider views we can take the field route to Whitewell (Map 21).

We go through the iron gate opposite the wood corner, and keeping left near to the road, cross level to a kissing gate in the wall (400m).

Up the path we pass to the left of the old quarry hole then level around the hill to another kissing gate in the wall (450m) (Map 16).

Up slightly on a path is another kissing gate at a wall junction (500m).

Straight on with the wall on our left we turn through a gate in the wall (100m).

Bearing round to the right and down a good track we pass the railings of the water installation to a junction in the track just beyond (300m).

We go left off the track and under trees past a wall end to a small gate and steps to the road, at the left end of a row of beech trees (100m).

Back on the road for a little while we go steeply down and sharp back to the right around the wood corner, past the Whitewell Hotel, and on with the river on our left to Burholme Bridge where we turn left (1km).

BURHOLME BRIDGE to FAIR OAK

Keeping left down behind the seat we soon come alongside woodland and turn left at the grass triangle with the old milk stand which is the first road on the left (700m).

Through the gate along the tarred road we pass Red Barn and on to New Laund (600m).

Keeping straight on along the road into the farmyard, we turn right, before we come to the house, at two tall cylindrical metal hoppers and through gates up a track by a stream (100m).

Over the culvert we bear left up the hill towards the right hand end of woodland to the top of the brow then parallel to the wood (450m) (Map 21). Here are some lovely views of the Hodder deep in its valley of trees. Around the shoulder of the hill (240°) we go down to the wooden stile in the wall (150m).

We follow the edge of the meadow towards farm buildings and through a gate in the fence (150m).

On by the wall and across the field towards the farm we meet up with a track alongside the wall and down through a gate (300m).

The track crosses a culvert and goes up to a good road where we bear left past the farmhouse (100m).

Beyond the farmhouse at a large modern farm building we turn right through a gate and keep alongside the modern building towards an old stone building set well back (70m).

We bear left around the end of the modern building, go through a gate into the field and then bear right to a stile and footbridge near the field corner (300m).

There are two routes from here. Either by a good track mostly, or by road all the way with perhaps an alternative via the stepping stones if we feel like it.

FAIR OAK to DOEFORD BRIDGE by track (Map 21)

Across the footbridge onto the road we go right about 20m then left along a good farm road to Higher Greystoneley (200m).

Straight through the farm keeping left of the farmhouse the track goes through a wooden gate across the field (250m).

It is a firm track now for nearly 2kms.

Through an iron gate into woodland the lane goes down to a shallow ford, or the footbridge to the right, and up again through woodland to the barn at Lower Greystoneley (300m).

We keep along by the small stone building bearing slightly left through a gate in the wall and on between hedges to a wooden gate (350m).

Straight on alongside an old hedge we pass Knot Barn and go along by another thorn hedge to the corner (350m).

The track goes across open field to a wooden gate at the corner of the field and along to the road (600m).

Exactly opposite we climb a simple stile in the hedge and we follow with the hedge and fence on our right to a stile at wooden rails, onto the road (500m).

The road goes along, then down, to Loud Mythom Bridge, *photo 78*, over the River Loud, and left at the road junction to Doeford Bridge (1km).

FAIR OAK to DOEFORD BRIDGE by road (Map 21)

Across the footbridge we turn left along the road and by trees then dropping past a stone barn on our left to a bridge (2km).

We keep along the road to Wardsley Farm and just past the farmhouse is an iron gate on the left and a bridge (200m).

This is the stepping stones route, but keeping to the road we go up around the corner and left at the junction, following the road along then down to Loud Mythom Bridge, *photo 78*, over the River Loud and left to Doeford Bridge (1½km).

When starting from the layby nearer Middle Lees it is easier to go back from here by road.

By road from DOEFORD BRIDGE (Map 21).

Up by woodland we pass a house then keep left at a fork by a stone barn (1km).

We keep along to the left at Middle Lees to the layby on the right (1km) (Map 22).

Or to the next layby on the left (600m) (Map 21).

By Stepping Stones from WARDSLEY (Map 21).

The Hodder is not always the quiet ripple of languid summer days. The stones can be dangerous if the water is up to the top and they should not be attempted in these conditions.

We go through the gate and over the bridge then bear right towards Stakes Farm to the River Hodder (150m).

Across the river and up the bank we come onto the farm track near the farmhouse and turn left along it past the farm (150m).

The track goes through a gate by the wall and climbs steeply up then levels above woodland to a sharp corner where we leave it to go left through an iron gate (350m).

Here we meet the path from Doeford Bridge.

By path from DOEFORD BRIDGE (Map 21)

The road climbs up by woodland to a white bungalow on the left (500m).

Here we turn left over a cattle grid and along the track to a sharp corner where the track turns left and we leave it to go straight ahead through an iron gate (350m).

| Here we join the route from the stepping stones.

From the gate at the corner of the track we go down a hollow grass track which bears right to cross a small stream in trees (200m).

Straight on we keep above the trees on our left to a wooden gate in the fence, under a tree (120m).

Through the gate we bear left towards trees and follow the fence through a gateway at the field corner, and straight on through another gate under a large tree (250m).

We bear right on a track to ford the stream and on up the track parallel to the Hodder which is on our left (250m).

The track becomes vague and bears down left, but we keep up well above river level, alongside a few thorns in an old bank (200m).

We keep along a hollow path passing a large tree on our right to a wooden gate at the top corner of the wood (150m).

We go through the gate and along with the wood on our left to the far corner (200m).

Straight on along an old bank (50°) we pass a single tree, then on a vague grass track we keep left of an electricity pole to a gate onto the road at the wood corner (500m).

One layby is just to the left, the other is to the right (600m).

For BURHOLME BRIDGE and WHITEWELL

We turn left along the road or through the iron gate across fields as described at the start of the walk.

WALK 45 (Map 20, 21) *Chipping, Gibbon Bridge, Greystoneley, Lickhurst, Chipping Laund, Chipping. 10½km or 6½ miles.*

3½km on road with some traffic. 4km firm dry tracks. 2½km mostly dry walking on grass. Easy walking by riverside woodland and pasture. In wet weather the paths can be avoided along tracks.

By bus or car: to Chipping.

Photo 78. Loud Mythom.

CHIPPING to LOUD MYTHOM (Map 20).

We leave Chipping down Talbot Street towards Clitheroe, and keeping right at the war memorial, go on along the road to the River Loud at Gibbon Bridge (2km) (Map 21).

There are good views of the fells to the left,

| If it is very wet we can continue along the road keeping left (1½km).

Over the bridge we go carefully down wooden steps on the left at the end of the bridge parapet and follow the riverside to a simple stile in the fence (250m).

On along the riverside we come to a footbridge over a small stream at the ruins of a stone barn (250m).

We can go either side of the river from here, the sunny side is perhaps the better.

Keeping along the near side of the river.

| We go over the footbridge and straight forward over rails in the fence to the left of the old barn and follow the riverside past the end of a hedge (170m).
| On by the river we go over a stile in the fence below woodland (140m).
| We then follow close to the river through the scrub and trees (200m).
| In the open again we follow the river then climb slightly just before a stream to go over a stile onto the road at the end of the bridge parapet (130m).
| Left along the road is the road junction at Loud Mythom Bridge where we turn left (70m). *Photo 78.*

The right of way is along the far side of the river.

We go over the footbridge and left to the river bank and easy stepping stones to a stile. Along the riverside past a few thorns we come to a stile in a fence (200m).

Alongside the river again we pass a small weir and go under the overhead power line (150m).

On over a stile at a fence and under a few trees we come to a wooden gate at the road opposite the farmhouse of Loud Mythom (400m). Here we turn left.

LOUD MYTHOM to GREYSTONELEY (Map 21)

From Loud Mythom Bridge, we go along the road past the farm and up around the corner along to a sharp right turn (350m).

The road soon comes alongside woodland on our right and half way along the wood side the road bears right and we go over wooden rails at the stile on our left (500m).

If it is very wet we can continue along the road keeping left to a lane at a house (800m).

We follow the hedge and fence on our left, straight to a stile in the hedge and across the road to a track (500m).

It is a firm dry track now for 2kms, to the road.

Along the track we go through a wooden gate and bear right through open field towards the right side of a knoll to come alongside a tall thorn hedge (650m).

We go on past Knot Barn and alongside a thorn hedge to a gate, then between hedges to a wooden gate in a wall (650m).

Slightly left around the small stone building, we go down a lane through woodland to cross a shallow ford at Greystoneley Brook or use the foot bridge hidden away on the left (200m).

Up again we leave woodland through an iron gate and go along the track to Higher Greystoneley (350m).

We keep right of the farmhouse through a gate and on along the track again to the road, then left and left again at the telephone box (400m).

GREYSTONELEY to CHIPPING (Map 21)

From the telephone box we go on and down to Greystoneley Brook again (300m).

There is a footbridge on the left and a path goes through Lickhurst Farm and across fields, but the ford is easier.

Across the ford, through an iron gate and another ford in quick succession, the road goes alongside the stream, then across a third ford and left up to Lickhurst (450m).

At the top of the hill the road bears right through a gate, avoiding the farm buildings altogether, and becomes a good firm track to a junction (50m).

Straight on, easier and drier in wet weather, the fell track goes over Stanley, left at Jenny Hey Barn and on to Chipping (5km) (Map 20).

The track to the left at the junction goes through fields and woodland to Chipping (4km).

This left fork goes through a gate with a notice which reads 'No Road Private' and refers to vehicles. There is a right of way on foot through the gate and along the track which goes through a gate in the fence and across a small culvert (300m).

The firm track climbs up then turns right and we follow it through a wooden gate, then on again with the fence on our left along a rougher section of the track to a gate (250m).

Along through trees the track improves, and at Park Style it goes left of the stone building and along the front of the old farmhouse (150m).

There are two routes from here. If it is wet underfoot we can continue almost entirely by track.

> Round to the right at the corner of the old house we go up a good dry lane between hedges, levelling out to a bend and on to a gate (250m).
>
> Turning left through the gate and with the fence on our left there is no track along through the gate in the wall and straight on to the wood (200m) (Map 20).
>
> Here we go right through a wooden gate to Park Gate, straight past the front of the house and along a good track again to turn left through a gate and over a bridge (150m).
>
> We follow the track on, turning left to Chipping Laund (800m).

The footpath route leaves the track at the corner of the farmhouse at the foot of the steep lane (Map 21).

> We go through a stone gateway on the left and across to a stile (234°) in the fence near an electricity pole (120m).
>
> On in the same direction towards a gap in the woodland we come steeply down to the wood and right to cross a footbridge over Leagram Brook (250m).
>
> Up left along the wood side on a path we meet the fence at the top and go over a stile up into the field towards the farm, to a stile by a tree at the end of the wall (150m) (Map 20).
>
> Over the stile we follow an old bank and keeping left of the woodland where it is rather damp through rushes, we meet the firm track to the right of the farm (450m).

This is Chipping Laund. We go over a cattle grid and bear right past the farm entrance along a good road, bearing left at the junction to follow the edge of the woodland (500m).

The road bends left at the wood corner to meet the main road over a cattle grid (300m).

For Chipping we turn right and right again at the War Memorial into the village (750m).

WALK 46 (Maps 20, 21)   *Chipping, Leagram, Loud Mythom, Gibbon Bridge, Chipping. 7km or 4½ miles.*
A road walk, most of it with little traffic. No climbing.
By bus or car: to Chipping village.

We leave Chipping by Talbot Street, crossing Chipping Brook and left at the War Memorial, then along by Leagram estate to a corner (1km).

Beyond the corner the road bends left by Throstle Nest then on to another corner (1km).

Just beyond we cross Leagram Brook and at the next house, opposite a track, a stile goes over the hedge on the right and a path follows a long hedge and fence to cut off a corner if we wish. The road continues to a junction where we turn right (600m).

Along by woodland above the Hodder we come to a sharp corner and on down to Loud Mythom bridge (1¼km).

Over the bridge we turn right and go up then along to a road junction (600m). We turn right again and along past a road end on to Gibbon Bridge over the River Loud (1km).

From here it is a level road back to Chipping (2km).

MAP 22 BASHALL EAVES

This is an area of quiet leafy lanes, from Middle Lees by Cow Ark and Browsholme Hall to Bashall Eaves. This little hamlet is on the Clitheroe to Slaidburn bus route and has a shop, a school, a few well built stone houses and the Red Pump Inn.

Browsholme Hall is a three storey sandstone building set in park land. It is the home of the Parker family who were keepers of the Royal Forest, and the family have lived here since 1380. The Hall was rebuilt in 1507 and given a new facade in 1604. It is open to the public on some days each year usually between Easter and October but not regularly throughout the year. Dates of opening are given in the local press and are available from the local Tourist Information Offices.

The land slopes south with deep wooded cloughs, to meet the Hodder which flows around the foot of steep land with long graceful sweeps of woodland. The footpaths from Lees to Sandal Holme and Masons, and across to Agden and Mason Green have lovely views of the Hodder Valley but both go over the stone bridge across the deep gorge of Mill Brook. Although these paths are open and still walkable from each end, the bridge, although some still use it, has been declared unsafe until it is repaired or an alternative crossing has been provided.

WALK 47 (Map 22)   *Bashall Moor Wood, Bashall Eaves, Sandy Ford, Braddup House, Hodgson Moor, Hare Clough, Bashall Moor Wood. 9km or 5½ miles.*
Returning by Talbot Bridge, 7km or 4½ miles.
A varied and interesting walk with a little of everything, quiet lanes through woodland, some riverside, and some moorland. A little climbing but worth it for the views. Plenty of birdlife in the woodland with curlew and lapwing on the higher land and peacocks for good measure. Mostly dry walking but one or two places where it is easier in boots.
By bus or car: to the junction of the narrow road with the main road near the south entrance to Browsholme Hall. There are a few places to park on the wide verges of the narrow road, but it is pleasanter to walk this road than drive it. There is also some roadside parking at Bashall Eaves, and the bus stops here also.

BASHALL MOOR WOOD to BRADDUP HOUSE

The narrow road leaves the bus route and goes alongside Bashall Moor Wood, turns right at a guide post, then goes on through woodland and down past a road end on our left to a corner (1½km).

From Bashall Eaves we leave the bus route at the junction by the telephone box and round two bends to a corner (500m).

From this corner there is a cul-de-sac road which takes us to Saddle Bridge. It is a very old bridge, hump backed and very narrow with hardly any parapet. There are two ways to it.

We go along the road about 200m to a track on the left to Clough Bottom. Down the track we turn right by farm buildings and along the far side of Bashall Brook into a field at Saddle Bridge (600m).

Or we may keep along the tarred road and over a cattle grid at Rugglesmire. Here we keep left of the buildings, leaving the farm track to follow the hedge and fence on our left down past the end of the modern building, through an old gate and left to go over Saddle Bridge into a field (500m). If this gate is obstructed it is simpler to go over the fence on our left and down the field.

We follow the brook side which soon spreads at a bend with an island of trees (250m).

We leave the brook here and continue in the same direction along the side of old thorn trees. The old hollow path behind the trees soon becomes a wet ditch. There is an iron gate on the right and we should go through it to follow the far side of the fence but if it is wet at the gate we might just as well continue along the near side of the fence which curves round to go past the end of the wood (200m).

Along the near side of the fence we shall have to climb rails at the fence junction near the wood, on past a gate to ford a shallow stream, then past another gate on the right to follow hedge and ditch towards the farm building of Sandy Ford (200m).

Before we reach the farm building we go through a gate on our right and follow along the other side with the fence now on our left, to meet a farm track just beyond the fence corner (100m).

We go right along the track which turns left through a gate and on towards Page Fold (500m).

The track goes straight on through the yard then left along a tarred road but if there are animals in the yard we can go left through a hurdle gate and skirting the farmyard meet the road through an iron gate just beyond the nissen type building (100m).

We turn left to the road junction at Braddup House (400m).

Returning by TALBOT BRIDGE

We turn left at the road junction just before Braddup House and follow the road along. It bends up to the right then left again to drop to Talbot Bridge (1⅓km).

The road bends beyond the bridge then on past Kitchens to a road junction with guide post (600m).

Up to the right and left at the top brings us to Bashall Moor Wood and Browsholme (2½km).

Down to the left brings us to the corner where we turn right and on around bends to the school at Bashall Eaves (2km).

BRADDUP HOUSE to HODGSON MOOR

Although this section is off the edge of Map 22 it is easy enough to follow. From the road junction we go straight on to the right of Braddup House, an attractive stone building of 1669. The road bends right and at the bend is a gate in the wall (not the gate into the farm) which leads us across a small field to go through another gate on a grass path through trees (150m).

This path was Whinny Lane but has been planted with young oak and beech trees, and become overgrown with gorse and broom so that it is really just a long narrow wood rather than a lane, with fields on both sides. It is a long steady climb from here and although we have to pick a way through the gorse at times it is a pleasant walk. The path becomes more distinct for a time alongside a deep clough on our left, and an iron pipe crosses to a covered reservoir. About 100m from here the wood thins out and levels a little to a gate in the fence onto a concrete road (500m).

We turn right along the road, through the gate, then just beyond we leave the road and turn left around the corner of the hedge. With the hedge and fence on our left we follow it up, cross a small stream, then on to an iron gate at the top (300m).

We go through the gate to another gate where a track commences (50m). The track keeps alongside woodland on the left and when the wood ends we keep straight on with the wall on our left (350m).

We follow the long straight wall, past Buckstall Farm towards the stone barn up ahead (500m).

At a gate we come onto a tarred road with a power line alongside it. This is Browsholme Road and we turn left along it. There are good views over the Ribble Valley and Pendle Hill as we go along the road to a modern bungalow and left towards Hodgson Moor Farm (450m).

HODGSON MOOR to BASHALL MOOR WOOD (Map 22)

We keep right just before the farmhouse round the corner of a small conifer plantation on our right and over a small stream towards the other farm buildings. We keep left of the buildings and left of the yard alongside following a track through a gate alongside a concrete wall (100m).

It is easiest from here to go immediately left through another gate and turn right following the fence and hedge on our right. We shall see a grass track over the fence which is the old route but it gets wet at the bottom with no proper stile. We cross a small stream and keep along the fence side to a gate at the end (350m).

Through the gate we follow the power line across the open field over the brow and down into Hare Clough to a wire fence where it meets the stream. Going down into the clough it may be drier to keep round to the right rather than go direct (350m).

Over the fence we turn immediately right to cross the confluence of the two streams and steeply up the clough side to level land above. We make for the buildings of Hare Clough Farm perhaps meeting up with the grass track to an iron gate (150m).

Through the gate we bear right on a good road keeping the fence on our right past more farm buildings and down around bends to a good stone bridge (500m).

On by woodland the road crosses a cattle grid and turns left through the woodland, then right past a woodland cottage to a guide post at the end (1km).

The road here goes straight on to the junction near Browsholme (500m).

For Bashall Eaves we turn left instead and go down through woodland past a road end to the corner where we turn right and on round bends to the telephone box and the school (1½km).

Maps of
BOWLAND

Scale 1/25000

| 500m | 1Km | 2Km |

| ¼ | ½ | ¾ | 1mile |

Public road, usually tarred.
Used by vehicles.
Right of way on foot.

Car Park   Cattle Grid

Road surfaced but not necessarily tarred.
Unsuitable for cars, or restricted access,
or private road.
Right of way on foot.

Gate   Unfenced

No right of way on foot.

Minor road in built up areas.

Track. Unsurfaced or grass.
Right of way on foot.

No right of way on foot.

Path, visible on the ground or waymarked.
Right of way on foot.

Path, not visible on the ground.
Right of way on foot.

Other paths. No right of way on foot.

Acceptable alternative route

Extent of Access Areas.

Access Strip

Map 5Km x 3Km   Grid 1Km squares.

Adjacent map numbers. 6 | 17
Overlap   No overlap

Boundary Stone .... BS
Guide Post .... GP
Telephone .... T
Letter box .... LB
Post Office .... P
Church .... +
Footbridge .... FB
Public Convenience .... PC
Cairn .... ▲
OS Triangulation Pillar .... △

Steep rock   Flat Rock   Boulders

Buildings   Woodland

Streams, rivers   Reservoirs

Waterfall

Contours and heights in metres.

· 384

350

Magnetic North | Grid North

Object

Magnetic Variation 7°W in 1982

Grid Bearing
Magnetic Bearing

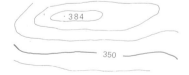

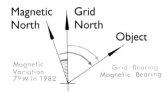

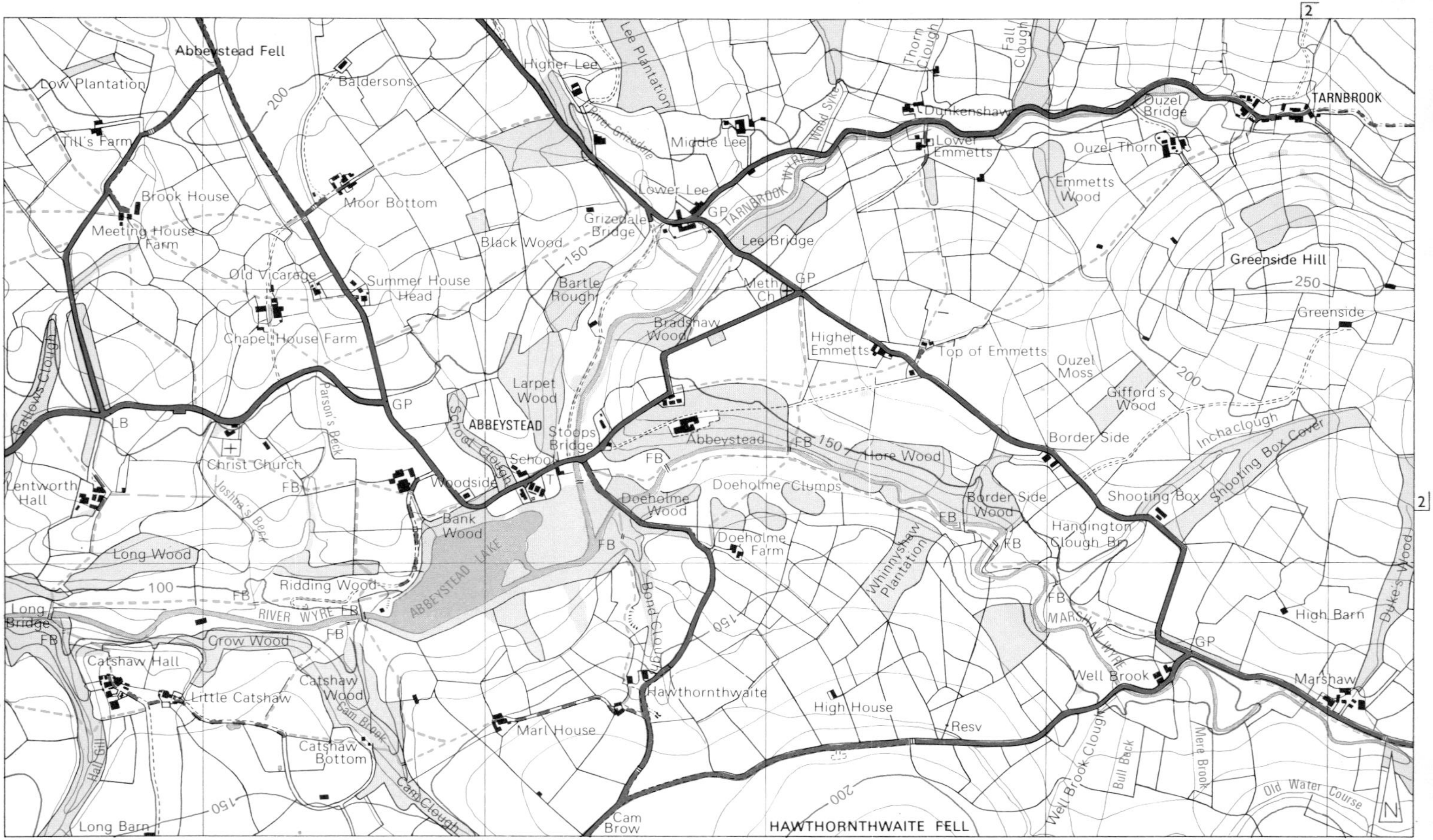
2
2
Abbeystead Fell
Low Plantation
Baldersons
Higher Lee
Lee Plantation
River Grizedale
Thorn Clough
Fall Clough
Dunkenshaw
TARNBROOK
Ouzel Bridge
Ouzel Thorn
Till's Farm
Middle Lee
Wood Syke
Lower Emmetts
Moor Bottom
Brook House
Meeting House Farm
Lower Lee
GP
TARNBROOK WYRE
Emmetts Wood
Grizedale Bridge
Black Wood
Lee Bridge
Greenside Hill
250
Old Vicarage
Summer House Head
150
Bartle Rough
Meth Ch
Greenside
Chapel House Farm
Bradshaw Wood
Higher Emmetts
Top of Emmetts
Ouzel Moss
200
Gallows Clough
Parson's Beck
Larpet Wood
Gifford's Wood
LB
ABBEYSTEAD
Stoops Bridge
Abbeystead
FB
Hore Wood
Border Side
Inchaclough
Shooting Box Cover
Christ Church
School
Lentworth Hall
Joshua's Beck
Woodside
Doeholme Wood
Doeholme Clumps
Border Side Wood
Shooting Box
Bank Wood
Hangington Clough Br
Long Wood
ABBEYSTEAD LAKE
Doeholme Farm
Whinnyshaw Plantation
Duke's Wood
100
Ridding Wood
Bond Clough
Long Bridge
RIVER WYRE
MARSHAW WYRE
High Barn
Crow Wood
Catshaw Hall
Catshaw Wood
Well Brook
Marshaw
Little Catshaw
Hawthornthwaite
High House
Cam Brook
Marl House
Resv
Catshaw Bottom
Well Brook Clough
Bull Back
Mere Brook
Hall Gill
Cam Clough
Old Water Course
Long Barn
Cam Brow
HAWTHORNTHWAITE FELL
N

MALLOWDALE FELL

Grey Crag

Queen's Chair

△ Grey Mare & Foal

560

550

500

ACCESS STRIP

Brownbank Guide

7

Woodyards

Harp Syke

Waterfall

450

TARNBROOK FELL

Long Crag

450

400

350

Thrush Clough

Gavell's Clough

Thorn Crag

300

Brennand Great Hill

Tarnsyke Clough

250

Black Side of Tarnbrook Fell

Small Clough

White Crag

TARNBROOK WYRE

White Side of Tarnbrook Fell

Swine Crag

400

Moss End

FB

Pea Carr Barn

Swine Clough

200

Tarnbrook

FB

Gilberton

Speight Clough

Deer Clough

350

Screes

250

Greenside Top

Rowantree Rocks

Greenside

White Moor

300

High Tower Plantation

Hind Hill

Pennington Wood

250

Tower Plantation

N

Tower Lodge

3

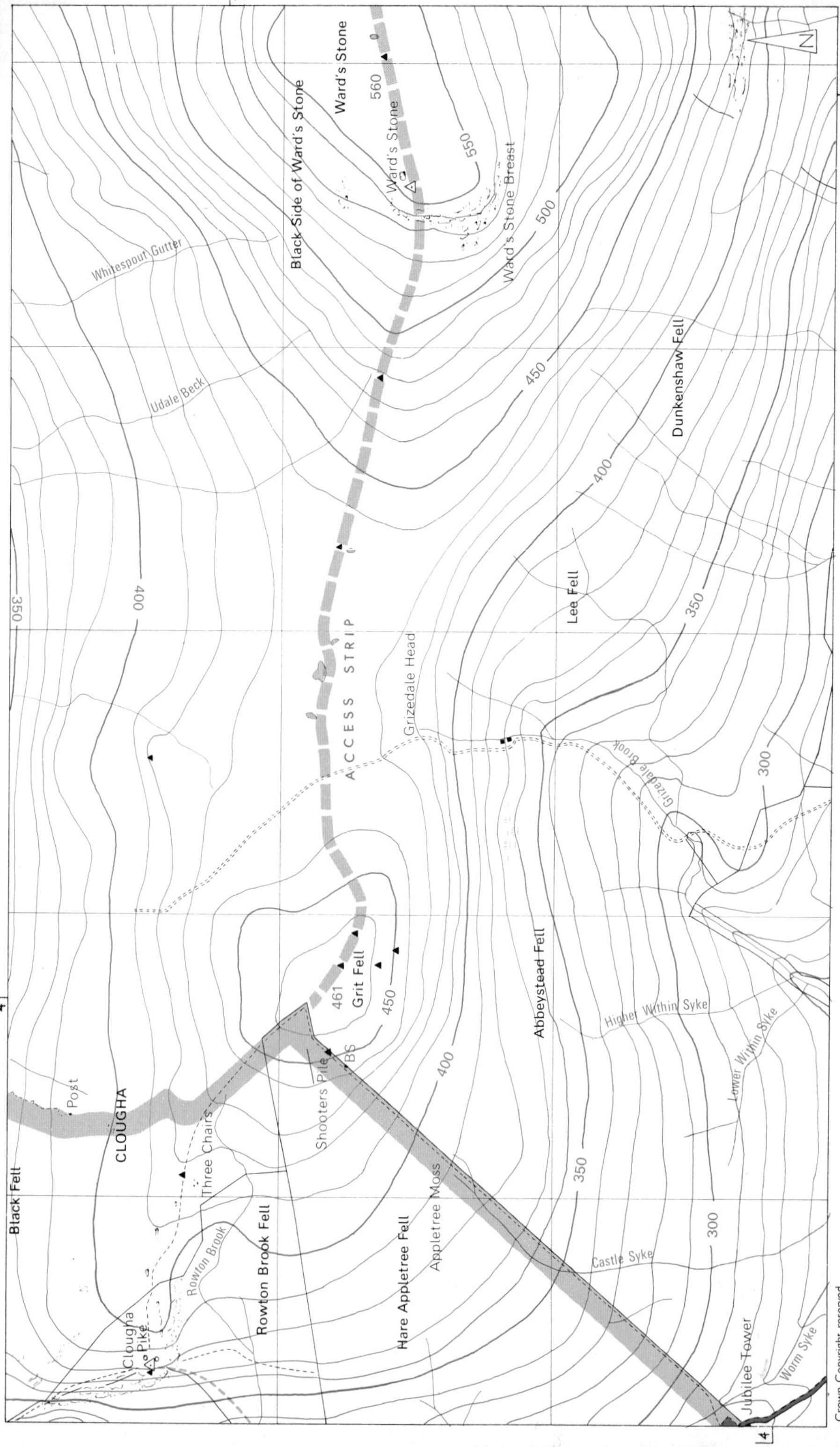

Ward's Stone
560
Ward's Stone
Black Side of Ward's Stone
550
Ward's Stone Breast
500
Whitespout Gutter
Udale Beck
450
Dunkenshaw Fell
400
350
400
Lee Fell
ACCESS STRIP
Grizedale Head
350
Grizedale Brook
300
461
Grit Fell
450
Abbeystead Fell
Higher Within Syke
Lower Within Syke
Post
CLOUGHA
BS
Shooters Pile
400
Three Chairs
350
Black Fell
Rowton Brook Fell
Hare Appletree Fell
Appletree Moss
Rowton Brook
Castle Syke
300
Clougha Pike
Jubilee Tower
Worm Syke
N
2
2
4
4

4

Intack House
Carr House
Long Ellers
Hollinhead Wood
Troulsmire Barn
Barnes Cragg
Little Cragg
The Cragg
Nicka Wood
Bark Barn
Field Foot Wood
Bellhill
Littledale Road
Calf Hill Wood
LITTLEDALE
Cragg Wood
Udale Beck
Rushey Lee
River Conder
Skelbow Barn
Sweet Beck
FB
Pillar
Windy Clough
Black Fell
Conder Head
Post
Dell Syke
Birk Bank
Bigg Lane
Fell End Farm
Fell End Fell
CLOUGHA
Rowton Brook Wood
Clougha Pike
Routen Brook Farm
Three Chairs
Rowton Brook
Rowton Brook Fell
Rowton Brook House
Shooters Pile
Grit Fell
461
Upper Browtop
Stone
Hare Appletree Fell
Appletree Moss
Hare Appletree
Damas Gill
Abbeystead Fell
Castle Syke
Higher Within Syke
Damas Gill
Westfield House
Jubilee Tower
Lower Within Syke
N

5

Cold Park Wood

Pyke Gill Wood

Hunt's Gill Beck

Alcocks Farm

Hamstone Gill Beck

Belhurst

Whit Moor Gate

Outhwaite Wood

Outhwaite

Wray Wood Moor

Back Farm

Whit Moor

RIVER ROEBURN

Barkin Gate

Bowskill Wood

Stauvin

Thornbush

Cowford Scar

Barkin Wood

R O E B U R N D A L E

Park House

Warm Beck Gill

Barkin Br

Podder Gill

Winder Wood

Harterbeck

Goodber Beck

Meth Ch

Low Salter

Hill Barn

Gill Syke

Goodber Common

Winder

Middle Salter

Drunken Br

Ford

Roeburndale Rd

Winderbeer Wood

Bladder Stone Beck

High Salter

Goodber Fell

Haylots

Hornby Road

Lambclose Syke

Mallowdale

Mallowdale Br

Middle Gate

High Salter Close

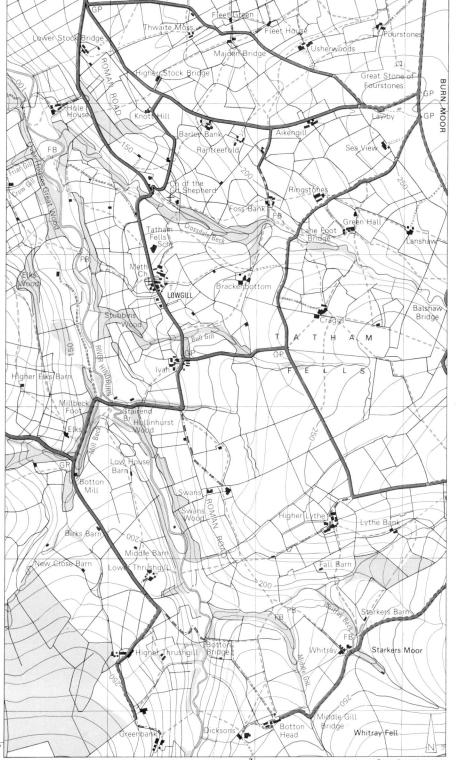

7

River Hindburn
Higher Greenbank
New Barn
Dicker's Gill
Dale Beck
Long Clough
Botton Head Fell
ROMAN ROAD
Ridge Clough
Greenbank Fell
Guide Hill
Thrushgill Fell
Summergill Fell
BS
Goodber Fell
Goodber Beck
Hawkshead
Salter Fell
404
Hornby Road
Alderstone Bank
Larn Syke
High Salter Close
RIVER ROEBURN
Waterfall
Bushy Clough
Mallowdale Pike
Marking Fold Hill
MALLOWDALE FELL

200 250 300 350 400 450 500

8

9

N

Fell End

Fox Clough

New Bridge

Smithy Hill

Swine Clough

Black Bridge

Waterfall

Gallery

Shooters Clough

Cleastdale Brook

Baxton Fell End

Quarries

Baxton Fell

469

Stoney Clough Head

Higher Stoney Clough

Saddle Hill

Reeves Edge

Raffen Clough

C R O A S D A L E   F E L L

Near Costy Clough

350

400

450

Bloe Greet

Snout Berry Hill

500

Little Bull Stones

Slate Delph Clough

Great Bull Stones

White Hill

544

Botton-Head Fell

500

Grinding Stone Rocks

Shooters Clough

ROMAN ROAD

W H I T E N D A L E   F E L L

Brim Clough

Burn Fell

450

400

350

WHITENDALE RIVER

300

350

Frog Clough

Sheepfolds

White Bank

Gutter Clough

FB

Whitendale Intake

250

300

400

450

250

300

350

400

450

500

9

CROASDALE FELL

WHITENDALE FELL

Croasdale Brook

House of Croasdale

Dyke Nook

Low Fell

Baxton Fell

Dane Hill

Black Brook

△436

△400

Meadow Clough

High Laithe

Whitendale

Calf Clough

Madder Grain Clough

Back Grain Clough

△450

Blue Scar

Middle Knoll

395

350

300

250

200

Clough Barn

Higher Woodhouse

Lough Beck

Dunsop

Hareshaw Brook

Procters

Dunsop Bridge

Gold Hill

Gold Hill

Harrisons

Grass Yard Barn

Laythams

GP

Davison's Syke

ROMAN ROAD

Burn Side

Burn End Laithe

Burn End

Dunsop Fell

Dunsop Brook

Burn Fell

Ox Rig

△431

Stone Haw Guide

Costy Clough

Little Costy Clough

Beatrix Fell

WHITENDALE RIVER

BRENNAND RIVER

Lower Brennand

Whin Fell

RIVER DUNSOP

N

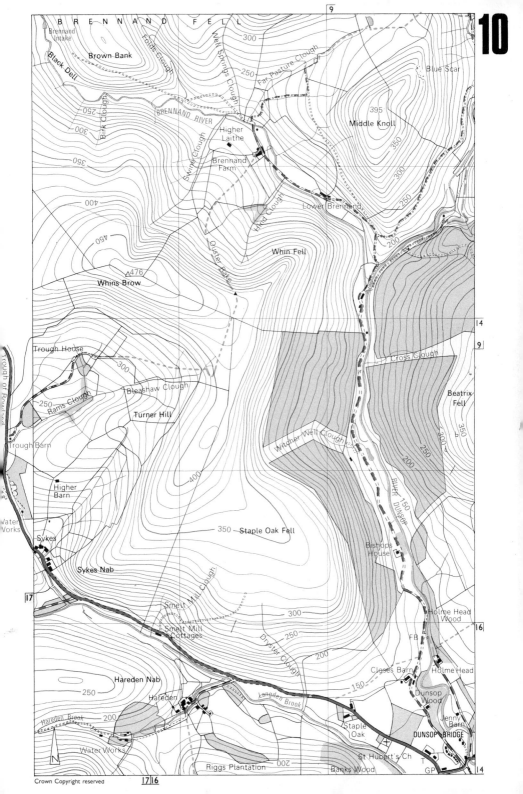

BRENNAND FELL

Brennand Intake

Black Dell

Brown Bank

Folds Clough

Birk Clough

Well Springs Clough

Far Pasture Clough

Blue Scar

300

250

250

300

350

400

450

BRENNAND RIVER

Swine Clough

Higher Laithe

Brennand Farm

Middle Knoll

395

350

300

250

Lower Brennand

Hind Clough

Ouster Rake

Whin Fell

200

△476

Whins Brow

14

9

Trough House

300

Bleashaw Clough

Rams Clough

250

Turner Hill

Cross Clough

Witcher Well Clough

Beatrix Fell

350

350

300

250

200

River Dunsop

Trough of Bowland

Trough Barn

400

Higher Barn

Water Works

Sykes

Sykes Nab

350 Staple Oak Fell

Bishops House

150

Holme Head Wood

17

Smelt Mill Clough

Smelt Mill Cottages

300

250

200

Dryster Clough

FB

16

Closes Barn

Holme Head

Hareden Nab

250

Hareden

Langden Brook

150

Dunsop Wood

Jenny Barn

Hareden Brook

200

Water Works

Staple Oak

DUNSOP BRIDGE

Riggs Plantation

200

Banks Wood

St Hubert's Ch

GP

14

N

17 16

11

Halstead Fell

350

Fair Hill

Dob Dale

Nursery Beck

North Field

371

Clough Hall

Whelp Stone Crag

300

Halsteads

Herd Hill

371

Old Ing

250

Lun Hall Beck

Tenters

Holden Moor

Dale House

330

Coat Rakes Br

Bottom Heights

Rigg Gill Syke

Cocklick End

Thorpe Syke

Geldard Laithe

Oak Clough

Hesbert Hall Heights

Slack

Bottoms

Hindley Head

FB

FB

White Hill House

300

Heath Farm

Bottoms Beck

Hesbert Hall

Far Barn

250

Waterfall

Hesbert Hall Syke

250

Higher Sandy Syke

200

Lower Sandy Syke

STOCKS RESERVOIR

Stephen Park

Moss End

220

200

High Head

St James's Ch

Park Beck

Cocklet Hill

240

Brock Thorn

N

12

Barn Gill

Picnic Site

12

Crown Copyright reserved

Picnic Site

210

Park Beck

Brook House

Dinkley Syke

Lower Stony Bank

Higher Stony Bank

Stephen Moor

Meadow Top

Champion

Champion

Higher Edge

Lower Edge

Black Moss

N

250

Anna Land End

Black House

Rain Gill

Lower Laithe

Standridge

220

200

Pikefield Plantation

250

Barn Gill

Frankland Laithe

Higher High Field

Lower Edge

Tinklers

Tinklers Brook

GP

13

200

200

170

New Laithe

Hammerton Hall

Farther Laithe

Lower High Field

Field Head

GP

GP

STOCKS RESERVOIR

Phynis

Phynis Beck

190

Woodhouse Gate

170

RIVER HODDER

Belt Sykes

Holmehead Bridge

150

New Br.

SLAIDBURN

PC

Meml

Hostel

Meth Ch

St Andrew's Ch

Sch

Croasdale House

Bond Hill

FB

200

200

Shay House

Wood House

Croasdale Brook

170

Lanshaw

Shill Brook

Simpfield

Myttons

Stone Bridge End

Townhead

Pages

New Laithes

Easer Beck Bridge

Elder Beck

200

13
14
9

11
11
9

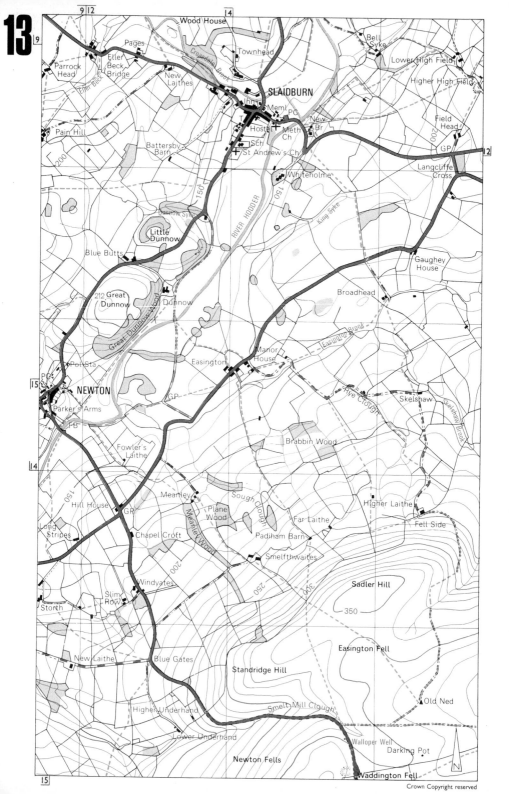

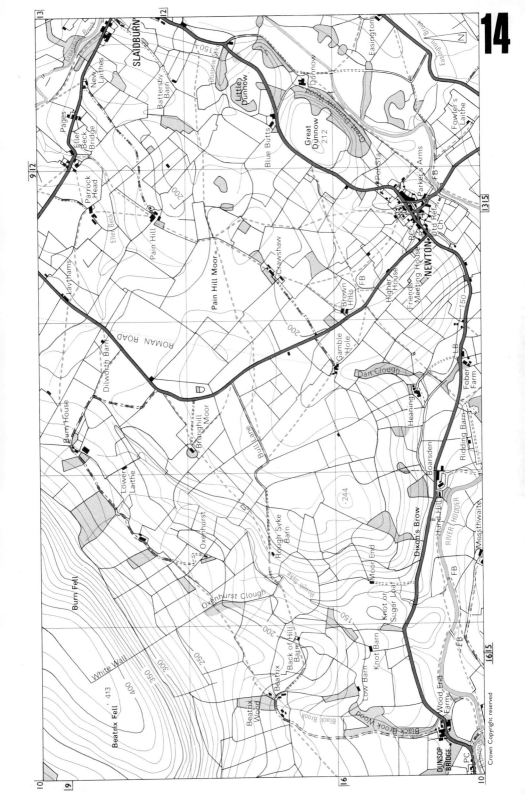

N

SLAIDBURN

New Laithes

Chipping Black

Battersby Barn

Little Dunnow

Easington

Fowler's Laithe

Dunnow

Great Dunnow 212

Holy Dunnow Wood

Pages

Fell Beck Bridge

Parrock Head

Blue Butts

Post Sta

Parker's Arms

FB

Old Rec
Ch
P.O
BCC

NEWTON

Crawshaw

Brown Hills

Higher House

Friends
Meeting House

Laythams

Pain Hill

Ellel Beck

Pain Hill Moor

ROMAN ROAD

Dilworth Barn

Gamble Hole

Darr Clough

FB

Fober Farm

Heaning

Ridding Barn

Burn House

Broughill Moor

Bull Lane

Lower Laithe

Boarsden

Dixon's Brow

Hund Hill

RIVER HODDER

Mossthwaite

Burn Fell

Oxenhurst

Rough Syke Barn

Rough Syke

Moor End

Knot or
Sugar Loaf

Knot Barn

FB

FB

Oxenhurst Clough

White Wall

Burn Fell 413

Beatrix Fell

Beatrix Wood

Beatrix

Back of Hill Barn

Black Brook

Low Barn

Black Brook Wood

Wood End Farm

DUNSOP
BRIDGE

PC

·244

·212

·150

·200

·200

·150

·200

·250

·300

·350

·400

10

9

9|12

13|15

16|15

10

13

12

15

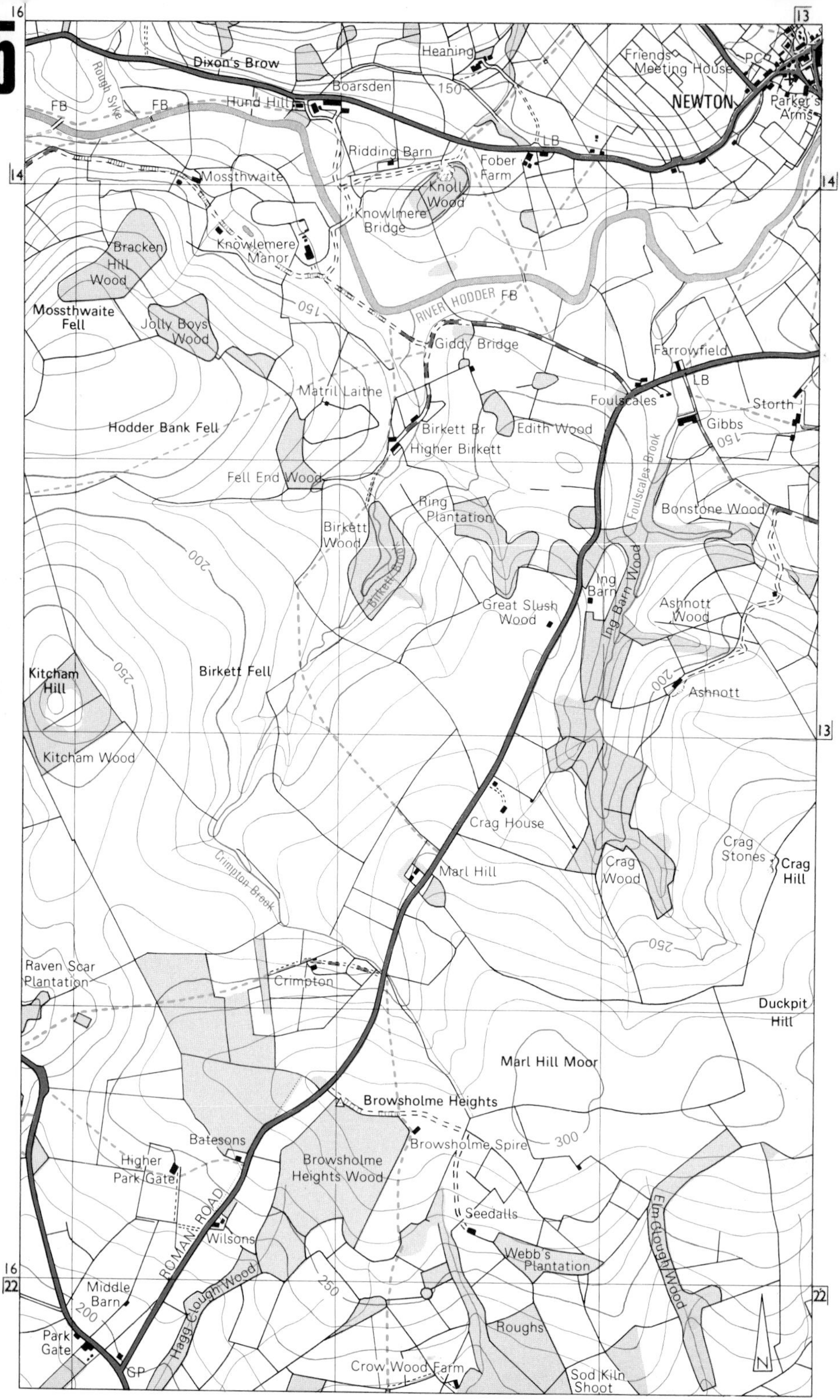

Dixon's Brow
Rough Syke
FB
FB
Hund Hill
Boarsden
150
Heaning
Friends Meeting House
PC
NEWTON
Parker's Arms
Ridding Barn
LB
Fober Farm
Mossthwaite
Knoll Wood
Knowlmere Bridge
Bracken Hill Wood
Knowlemere Manor
Mossthwaite Fell
Jolly Boys Wood
RIVER HODDER
FB
Giddy Bridge
Farrowfield
LB
Matril Laithe
Foulscales
Storth
Hodder Bank Fell
Birkett Br
Higher Birkett
Edith Wood
Gibbs
Foulscales Brook
Fell End Wood
Ring Plantation
Bonstone Wood
Birkett Wood
Birkett Clough
200
Ing Barn
Ing Barn Wood
Great Slush Wood
Ashnott Wood
Kitcham Hill
250
Birkett Fell
Ashnott
Kitcham Wood
Crag House
Crimpton Brook
Marl Hill
Crag Wood
Crag Stones
Crag Hill
Raven Scar Plantation
Crimpton
Duckpit Hill
Marl Hill Moor
Browsholme Heights
Batesons
Browsholme Spire
300
Higher Park Gate
Browsholme Heights Wood
ROMAN ROAD
Seedalls
Wilsons
Webb's Plantation
Elm Clough Wood
Middle Barn
Hagg Clough Wood
Roughs
Park Gate
CP
Crow Wood Farm
Sod Kiln Shoot
N
16
13
14
22

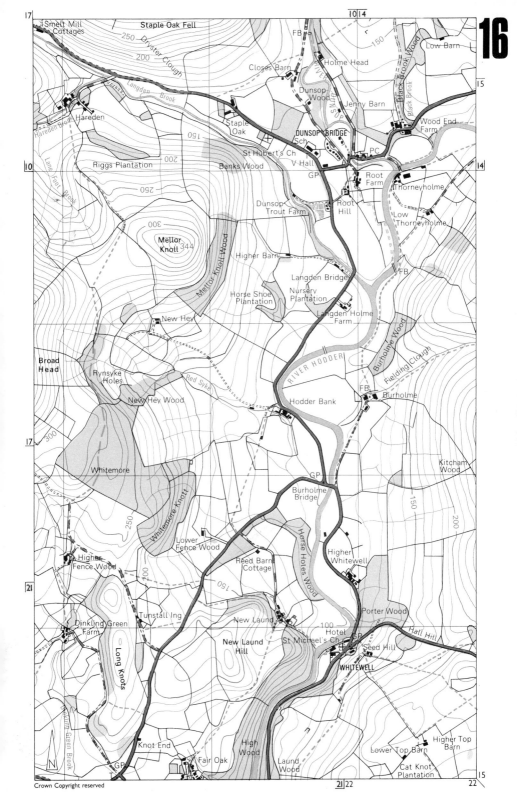

Smelt Mill Cottages
Staple Oak Fell
Dryster Clough
250
200
FB
150
Low Barn
Closes Barn
Holme Head
Black Brook Wood
Dunsop Wood
Jenny Barn
Black Brook
Wood End Farm
Langden Brook
Langden Brook
Hareden
Hareden Brook
150
Staple Oak
DUNSOP BRIDGE
Sch
PC
Root Farm
Thorneyholme
Lane Trout Brook
10
St Hubert's Ch
V Hall
GP
14
Riggs Plantation
Banks Wood
200
Root Hill
Low Thorneyholme
250
Dunsop Trout Farm
Root Hill
300
Mellor Knoll
344
Higher Barn
Langden Bridge
FB
Mellor Knoll Wood
Horse Shoe Plantation
Nursery Plantation
New Hey
Langden Holme Farm
Burholme Wood
Broad Head
Rynsyke Holes
Red Syke
RIVER HODDER
Fielding Clough
17
300
New Hey Wood
Hodder Bank
FB
Burholme
Kitcham Wood
Whitemore
150
GP
Burholme Bridge
200
250
Whitemore Knott
Lower Fence Wood
Horse Holes Wood
Higher Whitewell
21
Higher Fence Wood
100
Reed Barn Cottage
150
Tunstall Ing
Porter Wood
Dinkling Green Farm
New Laund
Hall Hill
Long Knots
New Laund Hill
100
St Michael's Ch
GP
Hotel
Seed Hill
WHITEWELL
N
GP
Knot End
High Wood
Laund Wood
Higher Top Barn
Fair Oak
Lower Top Barn
Cat Knot Plantation
15
Crown Copyright reserved
21 22
22

17

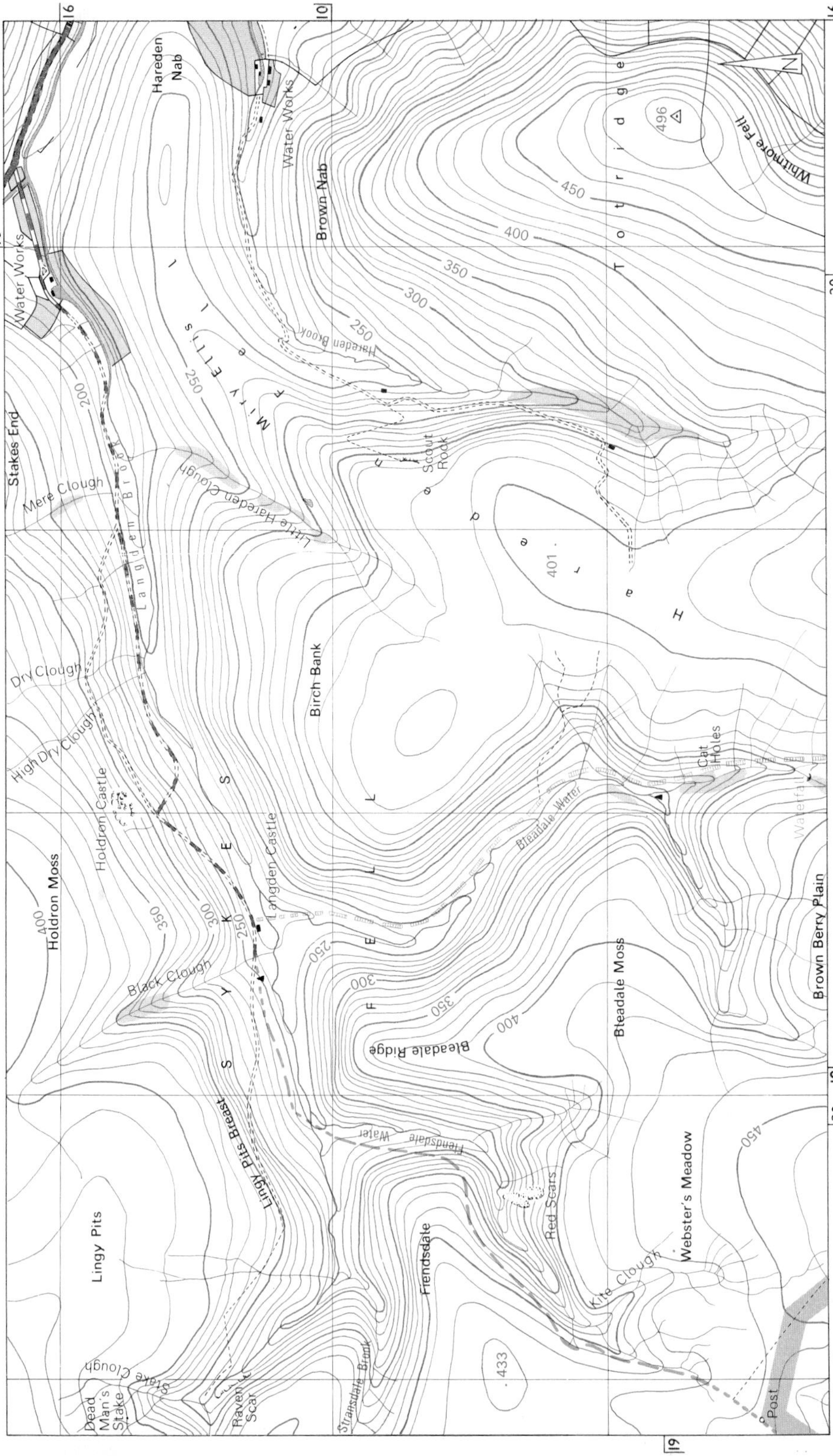

Hareden Nab
Water Works
Water Works
Brown Nab
Totridge
496
Whitmore Fell
450
400
350
300
250
Hareden Brook
Mirk Fells
Stakes End
200
Mere Clough
Langden Brook
Little Hareden Clough
Scout Rock
Hand Fell
401
Dry Clough
High Dry Clough
Birch Bank
Holdron Castle
Langden Castle
Cat Holes
Bleadale Water
Waterfall
Holdron Moss
Black Clough
Bleadale Ridge
Bleadale Moss
Brown Berry Plain
Fell Skyes
Lingy Pits Breast
Fiendsdale Water
Red Scars
Webster's Meadow
Lingy Pits
Fiendsdale
Kite Clough
Stake Clough
Dead Man's Stake
Raven Scar
Stransdale Brook
433
Post
10
16
19
20

N

19

19

Holme House
Hazelhurst
FB
FB
Admarsh Barn Farm
Vicarage Farm
St Eadmer's Ch
BLEASDALE
School
T
Higher Brock
Wickins Lane End
P
Brock Mill

Clough Heads Wood
Clough Heads Bridge
Clough Heads Brook
Brooks
Weaver's Farm
New House
Gill Barn
FB
Gill Barn Clough
RIVER BROCK
Jack Anderson Br
Bent Wood
Moss Side
150
Moss Wood
Brickyard Wood
Lodge Wood
Clough Heads
Bleasdale Lower
Winshape Brook
Broadgate Wood
Broadgate Meadow Wood
Brock Close
Winshape Wood
Fell Plantation
Fell End
Stang Yule
250
300
Oakenclough Fell
Broadgate Meadow Wood
Tootal Hall
Long Wood
High Moor
Broadgate
GP
FB
200
Huds Brook
Huds Brook Plantation
Moor Cock Inn
GP
Long House
Rough Moor
Landskill
Vicarage
Huds Brook Farm
Butt Hill
GP
Peacock Hill
Cobble Hey
150
Infield House
Bank Wood
Kelbrick Farm
St John the Evangelist Ch
Church Wood
CALDER VALE
Cobble Hey Wood
Keighley's Wood
200
150
Vale House
Shaw's Wood
Tongue Leaf Wood
Calder Vale
Sullom Wood
RIVER CALDER
100
167
Sullom High Wood

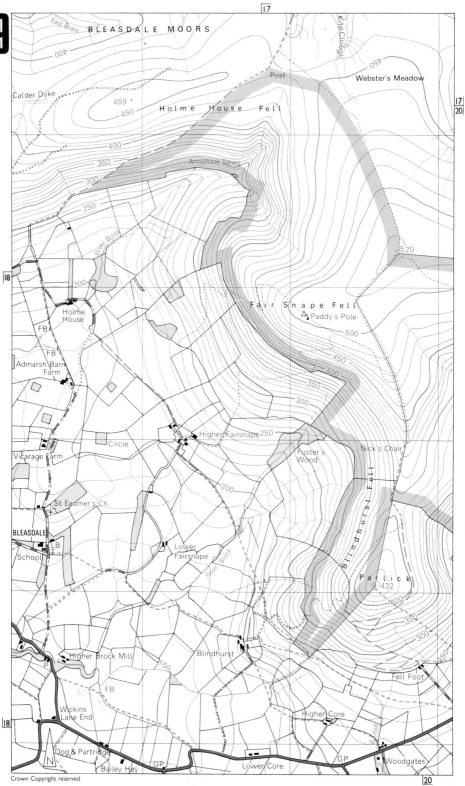

19

BLEASDALE MOORS

East Brain

Kite Clough

Calder Dyke

459

Holme House Fell

Webster's Meadow

Post

Arrowbank Spring

River Brock

520

Holme House

FB

FB

Admarsh Barn Farm

Fair Snape Fell

Paddy's Pole

500

Circle

Higher Fairsnape

Poster's Wood

Nick's Chair

Vicarage Farm

St Eadmer's Ch

BLEASDALE

LB

School

Lower Fairsnape

River Brock

Blindhurst Fell

Parlick

432

Higher Brock Mill

FB

Blindhurst

Fell Foot

Wickins Lane End

Higher Core

Dog & Partridge

N

Bailey Hey

GP

Lower Core

GP

Woodgates

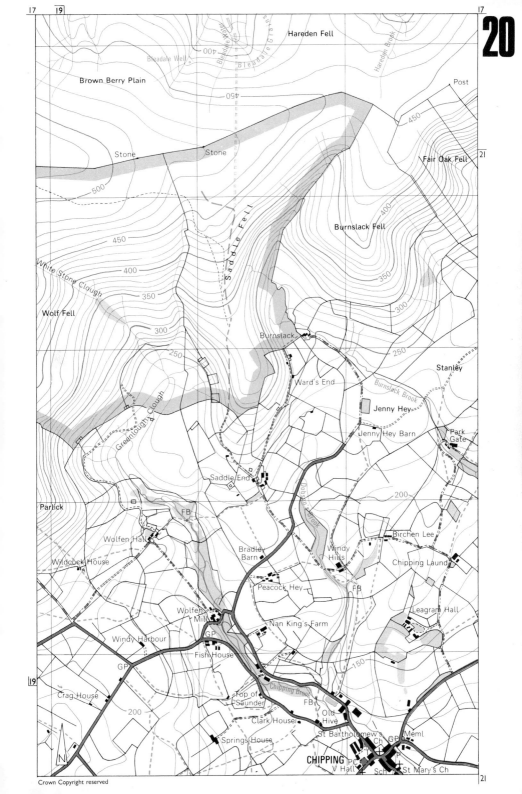

Hareden Fell

Bleadale Well

Brown Berry Plain

Post

400

450

Stone   Stone

Fair Oak Fell

500

21

450

Saddle Fell

Burnslack Fell

450

White Stone Clough

400

400

350

350

Wolf Fell

300

300

250

Burnslack

Stanley

250

Greenough d Clough

Ward's End

Burnslack Brook

Jenny Hey

Jenny Hey Barn

Park Gate

Saddle End

200

Parlick

FB

Dobson Brook

Birchen Lee

Wolfen Hall

Bradley Barn

Windy Hills

Chipping Laund

Wildcock House

Peacock Hey

FB

Leagram Hall

Wolfen Mill

Nan King's Farm

Windy Harbour

GP

Fish House

150

GP

Crag House

200

Top of Saunder

Chipping Brook

FB

Old Hive

Clark House

Springs House

St Bartholomew's Ch

GP Meml

CHIPPING

PO

V Hall   Sch   St Mary's Ch

N

21

Crown Copyright reserved

17   19

17

19

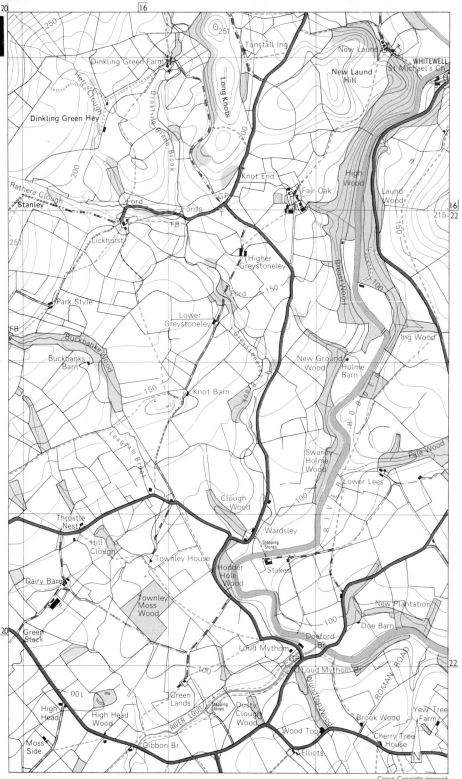

21

20

16

250

251

Tunstall Ing

New Laund

WHITEWELL
St Michael's Ch

Dinkling Green Farm

New Laund
Hill

Dinkling Green Hey

Long Knots

200

Knot End

High
Wood

Laund
Wood

Fair Oak

16
215-22

Rathera Clough
Stanley

Ford

Fords

GP
T

150

251

Lickhurst

F B

Higher
Greystoneley

Breast Wood

100

Park Style

Ford

150

Lower
Greystoneley

Ing Wood

F B

Buckbanks Wood

New Ground
Wood

Holme
Barn

Buckbanks
Barn

150

Knot Barn

RIVER HODDER

Leagram Brook

Swaney
Holme
Wood

Pale Wood

Clough
Wood

100

Lower Lees

Throstle
Nest

Wardsley

Stepping
Stones

Hill
Clough

Townley House

Stakes

New Plantation

Dairy Barn

Hodder
Hole
Wood

100

Doe Barn

Townley
Moss
Wood

Doeford
Br

Green
Stack

100

Loud Mythom

GP

Loud Mythom Br

100

Green
Lands

Stepping
Stones

Dusty
Clough
Wood

ROMAN ROAD

22

High
Head

High Head
Wood

Wood Top Wood

Brook Wood

Yew Tree
Farm

Moss
Side

Gibbon Br

RIVER LOUD

Wood Top

Cherry Tree
House

Elliots

N

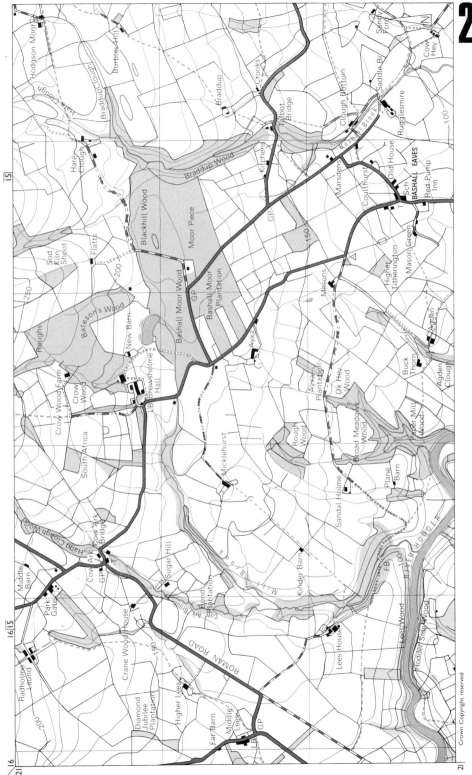

22

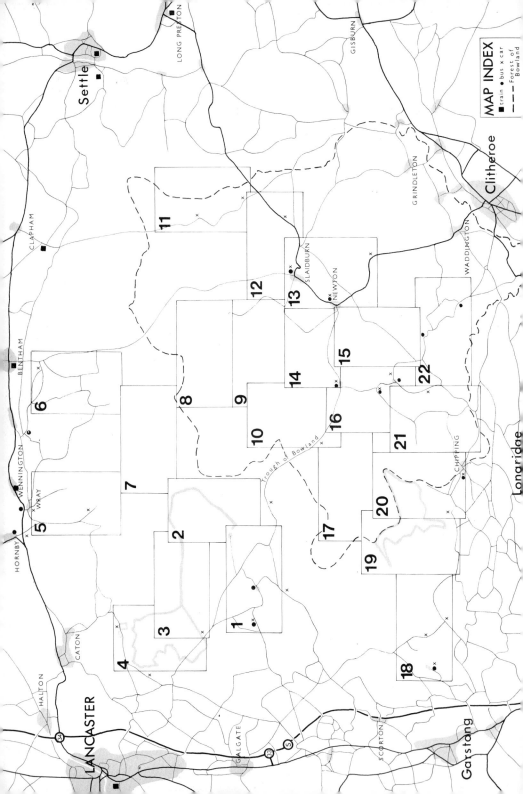

MAP INDEX

■ train ● bus x car

--- Forest of Bowland